INDEXATION OF PENSION
AND OTHER BENEFITS

Pension Research Council

Other Publications of the
PENSION RESEARCH COUNCIL

Indexation of Pension and Other Benefits

ROBERT J. MYERS
Professor of Actuarial Science
Temple University

Published for the
Pension Research Council
Wharton School
University of Pennsylvania

by

RICHARD D. IRWIN, INC.   Homewood, Illinois   60430
Irwin-Dorsey Limited   Georgetown, Ontario   L7G 4B3

ISBN 0-256-02118-X
Library of Congress Catalog Card No. 78–059212
Printed in the United States of America

1 2 3 4 5 6 7 8 9 0 MP 5 4 3 2 1 0 9 8

PENSION RESEARCH COUNCIL

DAN M. McGILL, *Chairman and Research Director*
Chairman, Insurance Department
Wharton School of the University of Pennsylvania

Robert A. Albright, *Assistant to Vice President and Comptroller,* U.S. Steel and Carnegie Pension Fund, Pittsburgh
Verne Arends, *Pension Consultant,* Milwaukee
Preston C. Bassett, F.S.A., *Vice President & Actuary,* Towers, Perrin, Forster & Crosby, New York City
Herman C. Biegel, Esq., *Senior Partner,* Lee, Toomey and Kent, Washington, D.C.
Edwin F. Boynton, F.S.A., *Actuary,* The Wyatt Company, Washington, D.C.
Laurence E. Coward, F.I.A., F.C.I.A., *Executive Vice President and Director,* William M. Mercer, Ltd., Toronto
John K. Dyer, Jr., F.S.A., *Independent Actuary,* Sanibel, Florida
Robert Ellis, *Manager, Employee Benefits,* Owen-Illinois, Toledo
Donald S. Grubbs, Jr., F.S.A., *Manager,* George B. Buck Consulting Actuaries, Washington, D.C.
Ernest L. Hicks, C.P.A., *Partner,* Arthur Young and Company, New York City
Russell H. Hubbard, Jr., Esq., *Corporate Employee Relations,* General Electric Company, Fairfield, Connecticut
Arthur Levitt, *Comptroller of the State of New York,* Albany
George M. Lingua, *Senior Vice President,* Citibank, N.A., New York City
Meyer Melnikoff, F.S.A., *Senior Vice President and Actuary,* Prudential Insurance Company, Newark
Roger F. Murray, *Consultant,* Peat, Marwick & Mitchell, New York City
Robert J. Myers, F.S.A., *Professor of Actuarial Science,* Temple University, Philadelphia
Therese F. Pick, *Director, Benefits Administration,* AT&T, Basking Ridge, N.J.
Bert Seidman, *Director, Department of Social Security,* AFL–CIO, Washington, D.C.
Robert Tilove, *Senior Vice President,* Martin E. Segal Company, New York City

v

Charles L. Trowbridge, F.S.A., *Senior Vice President*, Bankers Life
  Company, Des Moines
L. Edwin Wang, *Administrator*, Board of Pensions of Lutheran Church in
  America, Minneapolis
Howard E. Winklevoss, *Associate Professor of Insurance and Actuarial
  Science*, Wharton School, University of Pennsylvania, Philadelphia
Howard Young, F.S.A., *Special Consultant to the President*, United
  Automobile Workers, Detroit

PURPOSE OF THE COUNCIL

The Pension Research Council was formed in 1952 in response to an urgent need for a better understanding of the private pension mechanism. It is composed of nationally recognized pension experts representing leadership in every phase of private pensions. It sponsors academic research into the problems and issues surrounding the private pension insitution and publishes the findings in a series of books and monographs. The studies are conducted by mature scholars drawn from both the academic and business spheres.

Foreword

With inflation proving to be an intractable problem in the United States, given the political and social constraints within which economic policy must be developed, pension planners have become increasingly concerned with the protection of the purchasing power of both accrued and accruing pension benefits. Various devices have been developed, basing benefits on the employee's compensation during his last few years of employment being a common—and very effective—approach to protecting the pension purchasing power of employees not yet retired. The most direct and effective method of protecting the purchasing power of benefits in payment status is to adjust them in accordance with changes in a recognized price or wage index. This technique may also be applied to benefits of employees not yet retired. As a matter of fact, the 1977 amendments to the Social Security Act provide for the adjustment of average monthly earnings, on which benefits are based, in accordance with changes in average national wages—a type of wage index.

This book concentrates on the index approach to protecting the purchasing power of pension plan benefits. It emphasizes the adjustment of benefits in payment status but not to the neglect of accruing pension credits. Since the index approach has been more widely used in connection with public sector pension plans, the latter receive what some may consider to be a disproportionate amount of attention. There are many variations on the index theme and the author seems to have ferreted them all out and described them in considerable detail. He includes Social Security, the Civil Service Retirement System, the Uniformed Services Retirement System, and other staff retirement plans at the federal level, as well as the social security systems of many foreign countries. He has made a valiant effort to discover—and describe—the various index approaches employed among private sector plans.

The author was primarily concerned with the technical characteristics of the various indexing arrangements. He gave only passing recognition to the economic and social consequences of indexing. He has not explored, for example, the implications of insulating a large segment of the population against the debilitating effect of inflation on their principal financial asset—possibly at the expense of other segments of the population. Will it weaken the resistance to inflation if a substantial proportion of the populace is protected against one of the worst consequences of continued erosion of the dollar?

The author is eminently well qualified to undertake this assignment. He holds membership in 14 different actuarial or statistical bodies in this country and abroad. He has the unique distinction of having served concurrently as President of the Society of Actuaries and the American Academy of Actuaries. He was with the Social Security Administration for 36 years, the last 23 (from 1947 to 1970) as chief actuary. He has served as consultant to 38 different countries on social security and civil service retirement systems. Since leaving federal service, he has served as actuarial and pension consultant to many public and private organizations in this country, including congressional committees. He was recently named by the House of Representatives to represent it on the commission to study the Social Security System (the National Commission on Social Security). He has been a member of the Pension Research Council since 1958.

As is true of all Council publications, the views expressed herein are those of the author and should not be attributed to other members of the Council.

July 1978   DAN M. McGILL

Preface

This book is intended to examine in depth the various procedures that are used to index (or automatically adjust or escalate) various types of cash benefit payments, both in the private and public sectors, to protect them against loss of purchasing power. This is a very important subject in view of prevailing inflationary conditions.

The presentation has attempted to be on a purely objective basis throughout, so as to present the facts about the various detailed approaches followed in different programs. The last chapter briefly gives the author's views, which are, on the whole, supportive of indexing. It is possible perhaps that the personal bias of these views has permeated other chapters, although this was not intended, but the reader should be forewarned.

The author recognizes that some may say that indexing benefit payments merely adds fuel to the fires of inflation, and that the real effort should be made to control inflation and thus not have indexing working in the opposite direction. Quite naturally, the author is opposed to inflation, but he does believe that those categories of the population which receive benefit payments that lend themselves to indexation are, on the whole, among the lowest in income status. It hardly seems fair for them alone to have to bear the brunt of fighting inflation (rather than the major group involved, active workers).

The author wishes to acknowledge with deep appreciation the valuable guidance and editorial review given by Dr. Dan M. McGill, the Research Director of the Pension Research Council, and also many members of the Council who gave helpful suggestions as to sources of data and as to the review of the document. He also wants to give special thanks to Mildred A. Brill for editing and typing the several versions of the manuscript.

Finally, a general note of thanks is extended to the many persons outside of the Council who gave information about the benefit programs with which they were associated. Space does not permit mentioning them all here, although throughout the text they are given credit.

July 1978   ROBERT J. MYERS

Contents

List of Tables

Introduction

The viability of a pension plan, whether it be a national social insurance system or a private plan established for employees of a single employer, depends upon whether, over the long run, it fulfills the purposes for which it was established. Certainly, the fundamental purpose of any such pension plan is to supply, in whole or in part, a reasonably adequate income for the beneficiary (whether a retired worker, disabled worker, or dependent survivor of a deceased worker).[1]

If prices and wages were to remain stable (or reasonably so), the benefit payable over the course of future years would maintain its same relative level of adequacy as when it was first granted.

However, if economic conditions are unstable or dynamic, serious problems can arise for pension plan participants if the benefit amounts remain fixed in monetary terms over the years at the initially determined level. Under these circumstances, if prices rise, the purchasing power of the pension declines and is eroded, so that the pension plan will not be fulfilling its function of providing a segment of economic security to the pensioners.

---

[1] In the private sector, it is usually considered that pension plans relate only to retirement benefits and not to disability and survivor benefits, but from a broad theoretical viewpoint this need not be the case. Social insurance plans do provide all three types of benefits, as do also plans for governmental employees (and, too, under ERISA private plans must provide certain survivor pensions).

A somewhat different situation prevails if the price level remains stable but the general level of earnings rises (as a result of general productivity increases in the country). Under these circumstances, pensioners have their purchasing power maintained, but they will not be sharing in the increasing standard of living in the country. Nonetheless, it can well be argued that this is not an unsatisfactory situation since their actual standard of living is maintained. Others argue, however, that pensioners should participate in the increased standard of living arising after they retire—on the grounds that they laid the economic foundation for the productivity increases that occurred after their retirement.

In theory, the opposite economic situation from what has been described above could occur—namely, prices and/or wages could decrease over the long-term future. Under these circumstances, quite obviously, the pensioner population would become increasingly better off with their constant-dollar pension. In fact, if both wages and prices declined, the pensioners would be favored relative to the working population. However, this situation has never occurred over a substantial period of years, and under present economic conditions it seems most unlikely.

Accordingly, it would seem that under dynamic economic conditions, pensions should be adjusted so that they maintain, at least to some extent, their purchasing power—or, going beyond this, maintain their relationship to the general earnings level. Perhaps the simplest procedure is to make ad hoc changes from time to time as circumstances warrant. This may or may not be satisfactory from the viewpoint of the participants because the beneficiaries have no assurance that such adjustments will take place. On the other hand, the sponsor of the plan is not saddled with any contractual or implied commitments to finance what may be the very uncertain, but high, cost of such adjustments. It can, of course, be argued that if ad hoc adjustments are made frequently, there is an implied commitment to continue doing so—and thus financing obligations are really present.

Another approach to adjusting pensions for changes in economic conditions is to introduce automatic-adjustment provisions. This monograph will be devoted primarily to this subject and will first present the arguments for and against such indexing of pension benefits in force.

Various theoretical methods of indexing will be presented, followed by a discussion of the actual indexing procedures in effect under various programs currently using this approach. Such programs include the U.S. social security system, various governmental employee pension plans in the United States, several governmental programs in Canada, social security systems in other countries, private pension plans in North America and other nations, and the pension plans of several international governmental organizations.

This monograph will be concerned primarily with the adjustment of pensions in force and other benefits payable during retirement and also with the adjustment of other provisions relating to the payment of benefits (such as restrictions on earnings). It will not take up, in any detail, the subject of how the initially determined pension is computed or adjusted so as to bear a reasonable relationship to the pay level of the retiree at retirement or during a short period of years immediately prior thereto. Such results are frequently obtained by basing the benefits on the so-called "final wage." This, for example, might be computed as (1) the average salary during the last n years of service, or (2) the average salary during the continuous n-year period of service during which the participant's earnings were the highest (which will almost always be the same as that produced under the previous basis), or (3) the average salary of the n years of highest earnings during the last t years of service, or (4) at the extreme, the actual salary rate at the time of retirement.

Still another method of updating the accrued benefit rights of a participant so as to provide a pension that bears a reasonable relationship to final pay is to "index" the past earnings record. Under this procedure, in essence, the earnings record is expressed in monetary terms comparable to the salary level at the time of retirement. Thus, for example, if the average earnings series used as an index for this purpose indicated that wages in 1960 were at only half the level of those in the final year of service, then the indexed earnings record of the particular retiree would show wages for 1960 of twice what they actually were.

The indexed earnings record would then be used to determine an average wage for purposes of computing the pension from the benefit formula in the particular plan. Such average wage would probably be some form of career-average wage, either based on the entire period of service or on a period that reflects the dropping out of a few years during which the indexed earnings were low as compared with the other years. Such an approach is followed in the social insurance systems of Canada, Sweden, and West Germany, and was adopted in the United States in late 1977.[2]

Another method of indexing of pension benefits can be used in plans which have detailed and specific job classifications with salary schedules that are changed from time to time. The actual salary received at each period in the past can be adjusted according to what it would be according to the schedule in effect at the time of retirement. Then, either a career average can be computed from the adjusted salaries or else some form of final-wage basis can be used on such adjusted salaries. In essence, this procedure is equivalent to determining the average grade and class during the averaging period and then determining the salary applicable to it at the time of retirement.

---

[2] See "Reports of the Quadrennial Advisory Council on Social Security," *House Document No. 94-75*, 94th Cong., March 10, 1975, for a description of the original proposal that led to this legislation; see Chapter 4 for more details of the provisions adopted. A description of the method of indexing the earnings record in the aforementioned countries can be found in the following sources: Daniel S. Gerig and Robert J. Myers, "Canada Pension Plan of 1965," *Social Security Bulletin*, November 1965; "Canada Pension Plan Amended," *Social Security Bulletin*, August 1975; "New Graduated Pension System in Sweden," *Social Security Bulletin*, November 1959; and Paul Fisher, "Old-Age and Sickness Insurance in West Germany in 1965," *Research Report No. 13*, Social Security Administration, 1966.

Arguments for and against Indexing

Although this monograph has the primary purpose of describing various methods of indexing pension benefits in force found in different systems, it is desirable first to evaluate the merits of such indexing.

There are valid arguments for and against indexing. No definite conclusion will be drawn here as to whether benefits should be indexed. Rather, the subsequent chapters will explain how indexing can be accomplished, given a decision to go that route. Actual indexing systems are described in some detail.

The discussion of the pros and cons of indexing of pension benefits in force must be considered separately for broad governmental social insurance plans and for private pension plans established by employers for their employees (including in this latter category plans for government workers). In some ways, the arguments are common to both categories, but there are some points of difference.

INDEXING IN SOCIAL INSURANCE PROGRAMS

Social insurance or social security programs are established to meet the broad social goals of a nation. Accordingly, it would seem that benefit levels should be maintained in real terms so that these objectives will be achieved.

Such a result can occur either through ad hoc legislation or, where permitted, through administrative action, or through indexing or automatic-adjustment procedures. A discussion of the pros and cons of indexing as against ad hoc changes in a social insurance system can best be accomplished by reviewing the debate that occurred in the United States in recent years. Automatic-adjustment provisions for the Old-Age, Survivors, and Disability Insurance program were considered in the 1960s and early 1970s, prior to their adoption in the 1972 Amendments to the Social Security Act.

The primary argument of those who favor indexing is that indexing would promote social justice through prompt and equitable realignment of the purchasing power of pensions. They believe that the ad hoc method subjects the beneficiaries to the arbitrary whims of Congress. At the same time, the automatic procedure would, if not overturned by politically inspired legislation, prevent unwise overexpansion of the benefit level by political competition at the time ad hoc legislation was being enacted.

Some who argue against automatic adjustment do so on the grounds that political forces in our democratic society will probably build up pressures so that ad hoc increases will be added to the automatic increases, and thus the system will inevitably be overexpanded. The proponents of indexing agree that this could be a potential danger, but they believe that this is a lesser risk than would be present under the operation of the ad hoc basis alone. This latter argument is founded on the thesis that with no fixed standard as to the magnitude of the benefit increase (as the automatics do provide), the ad hoc procedure throws the debate into the political arena with no sound guidelines. As a result, overly large increases are likely under the resulting political bargaining.

The foregoing counterargument seems to be accepted by another group of opponents of the automatics. This group is in favor of substantial expansion of the benefit level of the program and sees the indexing procedure as being a straitjacket on the benefit level. Accordingly, they oppose the automatics at the present time, although they would favor them in the future after benefits have reached a level that they believe to be appropriate.

Quite obviously, the views of the groups described in the preceding paragraphs as to what would result if automatics were instituted are diametrically opposed. Both cannot be right! Certainly, if one is correct and the situation that they fear actually occurs, the other will be wrong.

Still another argument against the principle of automatic adjustments under social insurance systems is that the timing of the increased benefit outgo, which could be substantial, might be harmful to the economy. Specifically, it is argued, the added outgo might come at such a time that it would exacerbate inflationary trends, whereas ad hoc adjustment could be timed to minimize the undesirable economic effects or even to produce a needed stimulus to a lagging economy. Under the indexing procedure, there would be no control over the timing of the increase, as there would be under an ad hoc approach.

The proponents of indexing counter the foregoing argument by raising the query as to whether the beneficiaries, many of whom are in the lowest income groups in the country, should thus have to bear the brunt of the fight on inflation. Also, there is some question as to whether we have the economic knowledge to be able to ascertain just when are the "wrong" and "right" times to have the additional outlays for benefit increases impinge on the economy.

Yet another argument against indexing of social insurance benefits is that for a given overall cost, the result is a loss of flexibility in program structure and design. Under the ad hoc approach, if a certain general across-the-board increase were desirable and feasible from a financing standpoint, it would be possible to redistribute this somewhat so as to achieve a desired improved benefit structure. For example, if it were believed that widow's benefits were too low relative to other benefits, the situation could be remedied, without overall cost increase, by having a slightly lower relative benefit increase applicable to other benefits and a slightly larger increase for widow's benefits.

It is also argued that indexing of social insurance benefits will mean that a large group of the population will be unconcerned about the effects of inflation and will thus not exert any pressures (political or otherwise) to prevent its occurrence. The same situation is, of course, also the case with regard to the indexing of wages in general or of pensions for governmental employees (who, it is argued, might otherwise take stronger action or make better policies in the economic area).[1]

---

[1] For a discussion of this viewpoint, see Keith H. Cooper, "The New Elite: Those with Indexed Pensions," *Benefits Canada*, March–April 1977.

A strictly "political" argument is sometimes made against indexing of social insurance benefits in course of payment. Politicians assert that they want to have the "credit" with their constituents who are affected each time that benefits are increased by an ad hoc change by their action and vote, rather than have increases occur automatically (with any credit going to the actuaries, statisticians, or administrators)!

INDEXING IN PRIVATE PLANS

Perhaps the primary argument in favor of indexing of benefits in course of payment under private pension plans is that thereby the basic purpose of the plan will be achieved—namely, to provide a retirement income that will enable the pensioner to maintain a certain relative standard of living. Conversely, the lack of automatic adjustments in the face of rising prices and monetary depreciation can result in failure of the plan to achieve its aims.

Moreover, the automatic characteristics of indexing will assure that the real value of the pension is maintained and is something that the pensioner can look forward to with some certainty. It will also assure that those responsible for the administration and financing of the plan will definitely anticipate—or at least be aware of—the cost aspects involved in carrying out their responsibilities.

An ad hoc system of adjustment of pension benefits in force could, of course, achieve exactly the same results as an automatic indexing procedure. However, such an approach would possibly not give as much assurance to the pensioner and would very likely not be adequately taken into account by those responsible for financing the plan when they review the cost situation from time to time.

Some of the arguments against the indexing of pension benefits in force naturally follow from the "pro" arguments just given. Those responsible for the plan, it could be argued, will not agree—and, in fact, from the standpoint of prudent fiscal responsibility should not agree—to taking on the quite uncertain, but possibly very heavy, additional financial burdens involved in indexing.

To answer that argument, which it must be recognized has substantial weight, one could say that, at least in the case of a final-wage plan, the sponsor has already taken on an uncertain financial burden. Therefore, the sponsor might as well go the whole way and have a plan that produces adequate "real" benefits, not only at times of retirement but also subsequently.

From a technical standpoint, the argument as to the heavy and uncertain cost of including an indexing provision for pension benefits in force can be answered in large part by the use of properly conservative actuarial assumptions in the valuation of the plan. Specifically, one approach that could be taken is to use a reasonably low interest rate such as 3 percent. Such a rate can well be described as the "real" interest rate, or, in other words, one that would prevail in a noninflationary economy.[2]

Such an approach might well shock some plan sponsors who would argue, for example, that current investment rates on total plan assets are averaging 7 percent and that new investments are bringing in as much as 9 percent. Such persons should be "educated" to the fact that the much higher experienced rates of investment return are due largely to inflationary conditions and that the excess thereof over a "real" rate like 3 percent is not profit to the plan or a method of reducing costs. Rather, such differential is needed to finance both the final-wage feature of the initial pension entitlement and the indexing of pension benefits after entry onto the roll.

It is important to note that the procedure suggested above runs counter to the argument that all actuarial assumptions should be realistic and each should stand on its own feet. The answer then would seem to be that realistic, consistent, dynamic economic assumptions should be used and that, correspondingly, automatic-adjustment provisions should simultaneously be incorporated in the plan.

In actuality, if a pension plan has been valued under static economic assumptions and a shift is made to dynamic economic assumptions, a margin (i.e., reduction in cost) will arise that can be utilized to finance indexing of pension benefits in force. For example, let us consider the valuation of a final-wage type of plan for which both the assumed rate of increase in salaries and the valuation interest rate are changed by the same amount—say, by adding an additional 4 percent per year to the salary scale and changing the interest assumption from 3 percent to 7 percent. The result will be a *reduction* in the cost of the plan expressed as a percentage of

---

[2] This point was made by Paul H. Jackson, F.S.A., in a speech before the American Pension Conference on March 12, 1974 (as related by Herbert Heaton, "An Indexed Pension Plan at Low Cost," *Pension World*, September 1975).

payroll if no provision is made for adjustment of pensions in force. Such apparent cost savings can be appropriately utilized for indexing the benefits.

Let us now consider the cost of a newly established final-wage pension plan under which pensions in force are adjusted at the same rate as the wages of active workers rise (as will be discussed in more detail in the next chapter). Such cost is approximately the same under dynamic economic conditions under which the general salary level (exclusive of merit or longevity raises) increases at the same rate as the excess of the actual interest rate over the "real" or noninflationary interest rate as is the cost under static economic assumptions. Specifically, the cost of such a plan relative to payroll is the same when a 4 percent inflationary element per year is added to both the salary scale and a noninflationary interest rate of 3 percent as it is for the static salary scale and a 3 percent interest rate. (The word "approximately" was used in the preceding discussion because, precisely, the equivalence would be obtained only with a static interest rate of 2.88 percent.)[3]

Thus, the indexing could be accomplished through wage changes without any increase in the relative financing of the plan being necessary if the dynamic economic conditions turn out to be as hypothesized. To the extent that the increase in the interest rate over the "real" interest rate is less than the inflationary element of salary increases, a higher cost in terms of percentage of payroll would arise for indexing of pensions in force by wages than would have been anticipated under static conditions. On the other hand, as will be discussed in the next chapter, indexing on a less liberal basis, such as by changes in prices, would tend in the direction of lower costs.

Those opposed to indexing of pension benefits in force may also argue that the plan sponsor has the responsibility for the retired worker only to the extent of providing an adequate pension as of the date of retirement and that whatever happens after that is the fault of the economy, not that of the plan sponsor. But such individuals would hardly suggest that somebody else should take over the responsibility of maintaining the relative adequacy of the pension.

The question then would remain as to whether it would be desirable for the private sector to relinquish this much responsibility

---

[3] Derived as follows: $1.07/1.04 - 1.0000$.

and turn it over to the government. Might not the next step then be a governmental takeover of what were previously private pension plans? This could be accomplished either through a second tier of social insurance benefits or the amalgamation of virtually all pension benefit protection into a greatly expanded social insurance system.[4]

Still other plan sponsors might argue that they cannot afford the additional cost of indexing pension benefits in force. They would assert that, in a sense, some of the excess investment income currently available has already been used up to reduce or else hold down the overall cost of the plan. Such a conclusion is unfortunate because action was taken in the past that should not have been. Under such circumstances, it would seem that the course should instead have been to reduce somewhat the entire benefit level so as to have the financing available to index pensions. Otherwise, the additional cost of such indexing should be recognized through the overall level of financing being increased. Quite obviously, the former course of action would be difficult to take from a public relations standpoint, while the latter course would be financially painful.

We now get to the real crux of the situation about the desirability and feasibility of indexing benefits in force in private plans. If this is done, it is apt to be relatively costly to the plan sponsor. However, the burden of such necessary additional cost can be significantly mitigated if properly consistent assumptions as to the rate of investment return are used in the actuarial valuations. Specifically, if no automatic-adjustment provision is included in the plan, it should reasonably be assumed that little inflation is assumed for the future, and then a relatively low interest rate (such as 3 percent) should consistently be assumed. In turn, the higher interest rate actually earned if inflation does occur will be of significant help in meeting the cost of any automatic adjustment provision adopted.

On the other hand, if general economic conditions are moderately or highly inflationary, and if no indexing or ad hoc adjustments are made, the growing inadequacy of the pension benefits in force over the years will quite likely result in growing pressures for higher governmental social insurance benefits. In

---

[4] This problem confronting private pension plans is by no means the only one. Perhaps an even greater one is the failure to cover a large proportion of the full-time work force.

turn, this will bring constraining and restrictive pressure on private plans. As a result, it is quite possible that private pension plans will be "damned if they do and damned if they don't." If private plans adopt such indexing provisions, they will be faced with serious cost problems. But perhaps worse, if they do not do so, they will be faced with extinction in the long run.[5]

In any event, the high cost involved in keeping pension amounts up to date with prices or other economic elements will appear under either circumstance. In other words, if plan sponsors believe that they cannot afford the apparently high cost of indexing of pension benefits in force, they may well find that they will have to bear such costs anyhow through the expansion of a governmental social insurance plan that follows this procedure and then assesses them in an overall manner with its cost.

An argument against indexing of pensions is made along somewhat the same "political" lines as was discussed previously in connection with social insurance. In one sense, both the employer and the representatives of the employees seem to have something to be gained personally by having ad hoc procedures rather than automatic procedures. In this way, each time they will get credit from the employees for their action, and it will not be the case of "what have you done for me recently" that might occur if benefit increases come automatically.

ECONOMIC LIMITATIONS ON INDEXING

The foregoing discussion has implied that in all equity, the purchasing power of pensions should be preserved in inflationary times (if financially feasible). There are, however, circumstances where such procedure would not be equitable.

Specifically, if for any significant period of time, prices rise more rapidly than wages, it would not seem fair to have the retired population favored against the working population. Geoffrey N. Calvert, a consulting actuary, has strongly made this point in differentiating between inflation that is imposed on a country from abroad (as was recently done by OPEC) or that results from population pressures

---

[5] For an excellent and persuasive presentation of this viewpoint, see Preston C. Bassett, "Providing for Inflation in Private Pension Plans," Presidential Address to the Conference of Actuaries in Public Practice, October 3, 1977 (to be published in its *Proceedings* for 1976–77, vol. 26).

and shortages of raw materials and energy as against inflation caused internally in a country by wage increases or monetary manipulation. Mr. Calvert summarizes his views in the following manner:

> I am not suggesting that pensioners should be exposed to those forms of inflation that result from excessive labor demands, the inflating of the money supply, or similar internal causes which are not imposed on the nation or necessary to its survival. It seems to me that we must begin to consider a form of adjusting pensions and other incomes that recognizes something less than the full extent of the changes in the CPI.[6]

---

[6] From *Social Security and Private Pension Plans: Competitive or Complementary,* planned and edited by Dan M. McGill (Pension Research Council, 1977), p. 77.

Approaches to Indexing

The indexing or automatic adjustment of pension benefits in force can be accomplished in several different ways. These various procedures, along with their rationales, will be discussed in this chapter only in broad, general terms. Not considered will be various technical elements such as the periods involved in determining the change in the index, the magnitude of change in the index before benefits are adjusted, and the time lags involved between the determination of the change and the actual effective date of the adjustment in benefits.

In theory and in logic, any indexing of pension benefits should operate in both directions, down as well as up, depending upon the movement of the index. In practice, however, from both political and public relations viewpoints, it is usually prescribed that adjustments will only be upward (if at all). Of course, under such circumstances, if there is a period when decreases would occur, any subsequent increase would be measured from the last previous adjustment and not from the low point of the trough that occurred subsequently.

Furthermore, as a practical matter, under the economic experience of the past few decades, any decreases in the index that would likely be used for pension adjustments have not persisted for a long period, and the index shortly rose again beyond the highest previous level. Accordingly, it might hardly seem worthwhile from a practical standpoint to decrease pension benefits by the indexing procedure, since this would likely have only a temporary small effect.

In the remainder of this chapter, the discussion will refer only to *increasing* future benefits by indexing, although of course this could readily relate to decreases as well if these were provided for.

Before the several different procedures for indexing pension benefits are considered, mention should be made of two methods that are frequently used to provide variable pension benefits. The hope of such methods is to approximate closely the benefit levels that would be needed to keep up with rising prices or rising living standards—or at least to move the pension amount in the same general direction.

One such approach is the variable annuity, or equity annuity, under which the amount of the benefit fluctuates (definitely downward as well as upward) in concert with changes in the average unit value of the investment portfolio of common stocks (or, in some instances, a designated mix of bonds and common stocks). The theory behind the variable annuity is that over a considerable period of past history, common stock prices have moved upward along with the trend in general prices. But there have been some periods when this general situation did not occur (notably in the past few years).

Another such approach is the guaranteed increasing pension, under which each year the benefit amount will be a prescribed percentage larger than in the previous year. Such an approach can well be guaranteed because it can be derived on a proper actuarial basis. Thus, for example, if the fund is expected to earn 6 percent interest and if its mortality basis is the U.S. Total Males Life Table for 1959–61, then a level pension of $100 per month for a man aged 65 can be converted, without cost to the plan, to a pension increasing at the rate of 3 percent per year if the initial pension amount for the first 12 months is $82.15. Such an approach, of course, gives no actuarial advantage to the pensioner, although it does recast the stream of benefit payments in a manner that will very likely come closer to approximating future changes in prices. The disadvantage, of course, is that the pension starts at a substantially lower level. Of course, such a procedure need not be done at the expense of the pensioner because the employer can change the plan to provide the same initial pension as previously and, in addition, can include this automatic-increase provision.

A modification of the foregoing approach is to have the annual increases be a prescribed percentage of the *initial* pension amount, rather than of the *previous year's* amount. The resulting future amounts are, therefore, lower than they would be on the "compounding" basis, and so the reduction in the initial pension amount to provide this feature is less. In the example given, the initial pension would be $84.32 instead of $82.15.

Neither of the foregoing two methods can properly be considered to be indexing the pension (although they do involve automatic-adjustment procedures), and we will now turn to several true indexing procedures.

INDEXING BY PRICES

The frequently stated aim of indexing pension benefits in force is to maintain the real or purchasing power of the benefits. With this objective, the pension amount is adjusted periodically according to the percentage change in an index representing prices. Quite simply, for example, if prices rose by 3.8 percent between two base periods, the pension would be increased by 3.8 percent beginning with a designated effective date.

The frequency of the changes and the lag involved in implementing the index can have a significant effect on whether the pension is really maintaining its purchasing power at all times during the period of pension receipt or whether this is done only at the adjustment points (if even then). Specifically, if the increase occurs a few months after the change in the index is measured, the pension will never quite have the same real value as when it was initially granted; and, in fact, in the periods between adjustments there will be further dips.

For example, if prices increase by 0.5 percent per month and if the adjustments are made every 12 months, but with a 3-month administrative delay, then an initial payment of $100 per month will remain payable for the next 14 months and then will be increased to $106.17. The latter amount, however, has a real value relative to prices in the initial pension month of only $98.52. In the month preceding the first adjustment, the real value of the $100 payment actually made was only $93.26. Then, in the 12-month period following the first adjustment, the fixed payment of $106.17 per month deteriorates in real terms to only $93.26 for the 12th month before being increased to $112.72 for the next month, which in turn then has a real value of only $98.52 (or the same as after the first adjustment). This situation continues throughout the remainder of the pensioner's lifetime, with the real value dipping after each adjustment before it is brought back to the same real value as it had after the first adjustment, which is some 1½ percent lower than the size of the pension when it was first granted.

Some might argue that the foregoing situation is not really inequitable to the pensioner. The initial pension amount could be said to have been developed with the thought in mind that there would be some temporary depreciation in its real value in the future. Also, it could be argued that pensioners are fortunate to have a reasonably good indexing of their pension provided. Moreover, active workers do not have their pay continuously kept up to date with rising prices, but rather wage increases come sporadically.

On the other hand, from a technical standpoint, methods can be developed to offset the cycles of drops in the real value of the pension as contrasted with its initial amount. A very scientific, precise procedure to obtain such a result can be developed, but it would be extremely complicated both to administer and to explain to the pensioners.[1] A much simpler and more practical solution to this problem, if it is desired that it be solved, can be developed. Specifically, the periodical pension adjustment would include a small addition that would be based on the time involved since the previous adjustment so that approximate retroactive adjustments would, in effect, be made prospectively. There would, however, be no adjustment made for the final period of pension receipt (i.e., when death or other termination occurs).

A specific example of how this approximate adjustment for lag could operate is given for a simplified case. Let us assume that the pension is $100 per month for the initial month and that adjustment is made every 12 months, with a 3-month delay before it appears in the pension check. If the price index increases ½ percent each month, then the first increase (6.17 percent) would be augmented

---

[1] For an intricate, but precise, method of doing this for military retired pay, see E. J. Devine and R. A. Kuzmack, *Integration of Military Retired Pay and Social Security Benefits: The Attribution Problem and Its Implication for the Private Sector* (Defense Manpower Commission, October 17, 1975).

by (*a*) the total percentage loss in the period that the initial pension was payable, spread over (*b*) the period that will likely elapse before the next increase will occur. Item (*a*) is, on an approximate basis, the 15 months involved times the average percentage loss, which is 50 percent of the first increase, while item (*b*) is the 12 months in the future before the next increase can occur. Accordingly, the adjustment for lag under this basis would be 3.86 percent (15 times one half of 6.17, divided by 12); in subsequent adjustments, the "past period of loss" would not be 15 months, but rather 12 months if an adjustment is made in that time (otherwise 24, 36, etc., months). The total adjustment would then be 10.27 percent (the accumulation of 6.17 percent and 3.86 percent).

A more specific aspect of indexing pension benefits in force by prices is the very practical matter of what price index should be used. By far the most widely known price index in the United States is the Consumer Price Index (CPI), prepared by the Bureau of Labor Statistics of the U.S. Department of Labor. This index, it is important to note, relates to urban wage earners and clerical workers.

Because of this specialized nature of the CPI, it has sometimes been criticized as not being applicable to pensioners. It is pointed out that the expenditures of a pensioner have a quite different pattern than those of an urban worker—for example, lower costs for clothing and transportation and higher costs for medical care. To a considerable extent, however, the higher costs for medical care for pensioners are offset by the comprehensive protection that they have under Medicare. Although there are fine theoretical arguments in favor of a separate price index for pensioners, in practice it would seem that even if it were developed, the results would not be too far different from using the long-established and widely accepted CPI.[2] Also, it is possible that if an index were developed for this special purpose, political pressures could develop to manipulate it so as to produce "better" effects on benefits.

The 1977 Amendments to the Social Security Act contain a provision that a newly established National Commission on Social Security is to study, among other things, the possibility of developing a special CPI for the elderly.

---

[2] For the latest that has been written on this subject, see Janet L. Norwood, "Cost-of-Living Escalation of Pensions," *Monthly Labor Review,* June 1972. Her conclusion, which is still valid, is worth noting: "Data are not now available to determine whether a CPI for the retired would differ from present CPI, and, if so, whether the differences would be large enough to affect annuity escalation."

The CPI is available for the total United States and also for 28 cities and metropolitan areas (on a monthly basis for some and on a bi-monthly basis for others). It is also available for certain subdivisions of expenditures, such as food, housing, medical care, and apparel. The index most likely to be used is that for all items for the country as a whole, although in some instances the CPI for the particular locality where the pension plan is located is used. Actually, the CPI does not vary greatly as between localities because it is a measure of relative change in each locality, not as between localities. Thus, for example, for May 1977, the CPI (on the basis of 1967 being 100) varied in the different localities only from 168.3 to 188.8; and 83 percent of the localities were within 5 percentage points of the national CPI of 180.6.

Beginning January 1978, the Bureau of Labor Statistics is publishing three CPIs, as follows:

1. The original CPI, which will be continued for only six months.
2. A CPI for urban blue-collar and clerical workers (the basis of the original CPI), but for a broader sample as to items included. This may be discontinued at the end of 1980.
3. A CPI for all urban consumers.

It would seem likely that plans indexing by the CPI will shift over to the all-urban CPI, with suitable bridging between the two series being readily possible. The U.S. social security program (discussed in the next chapter) would, under legislation proposed by the Carter Administration, use this new CPI as the basis for its automatic adjustment of benefits in course of payment.

As indicated in the previous chapter, such indexing by the CPI could readily be financed without any increase in cost (as a percentage of payroll) if the inflation in salaries was no more than the rise in the interest rate due to inflation as compared with the cost anticipated under static economic conditions. In fact, such a "no cost" situation would be present even if the rise in interest rates is not quite as large as the inflation in salaries (assuming that prices rise less rapidly than salaries).

Recently, Geoffrey N. Calvert, F.I.A. (an early advocate of full automatic adjustments of pensions in course of payment for changes in the cost of living[3]), has advocated a somewhat different

---

[3] See, for example, his paper, "Cost-of-Living Pension Plan," *Harvard Business Review*, September–October 1954.

approach than keeping pension amounts constant in real terms.[4] In brief, based on analysis of a small number of Canadian families headed by individuals aged 65 or over, he now concludes that only part of retirement income (about 40 percent) needs to have its purchasing power sustained as age advances and that the remainder need not be because the financial needs of people lessen with time. Accordingly, he concludes that total retirement income should be indexed *less* than the full extent of price changes, which could perhaps be accomplished by escalating such total income at a rate lower than CPI changes or by fully indexing only a portion of such total income. In practice, this could be done by full indexing of social insurance benefits and little (or no) indexing of private pensions.

INDEXING BY WAGES

Some would argue that indexing pension benefits in force solely by prices does not give adequate social justice to the beneficiaries. Thus, although it is true that their real purchasing power is maintained, no recognition is included for the rising standards of living of the country as a result of productivity increases. Roughly, it may be stated that the remuneration of workers (including both cash earnings and fringe benefits) tends to increase more rapidly than prices to the extent that productivity gains occur—and as a result, standards of living rise.

Philosophically, it can be argued that the retired should share in the productivity gains currently being made by the active workers. Or, conversely, it can be argued with equal logic that current productivity gains should only go to current workers. If the latter approach is taken, then indexing of pension benefits in force by prices is the answer. But if the former philosophy is embraced, then the current productivity gains should be shared by the active workers with the retired workers by indexing the pensions by wages—and at the same time the cost thereof would be met by smaller increases in real wages for the active workers.

Over the long pull, wages have generally risen more rapidly than prices, with the average annual differential being perhaps 2 to 2½ percent. In some recent years, however, the situation was just the

---

[4] See his book, *Pensions and Survival* (Toronto: Maclean-Hunter Limited, 1977), chap. 4.

reverse; and prices rose more rapidly than wages. It would seem that over the long-range future, the situation will switch back to that which prevailed in the more distant past. However, there are reasons to believe that the differential of wage increases over price increases may be much smaller than the 2 to 2½ percent per year that prevailed in the past.

In any event, it would seem that pensioners would be better off with indexing by wages than indexing by prices. Of course, this means higher pension costs to be paid by the plan and thus, indirectly, by the current work force.

Although it is very unlikely that over a long period of time wages will increase less rapidly than prices, it is a possible situation. Under such circumstances, it would hardly seem reasonable or acceptable to the working population if pensioners had their benefits increased more rapidly than wages so that these benefits would maintain their real purchasing power, whereas wages did not. Under such most unlikely economic circumstances, it would seem that any system of indexing pensions by prices should have a ceiling imposed in terms of changes in a relevant wage index. Quite obviously, this restrictive approach should be taken only after a long-term trend had become apparent. It would not be fair to index on a year-by-year basis by the *lower* of price increases or wage increases, just as it would not be fair to give pensioners "the best of all worlds" by indexing on a year-by-year basis by the *higher* of price or wage increases.

As discussed in the previous chapter, such indexing by wages could be financed at exactly the same cost (relative to payroll) as would be expected under static economic conditions if the increase in the interest rate over the "real" rate is the same as the relative inflation in salaries. Such a relationship is quite likely to occur. Financial conservatism, however, might dictate the indexing of pension benefits in course of payment by prices because of the likely margin of safety contained therein as against indexing by wages.

INDEXING BY JOB CLASSIFICATION

Another method of indexing pension benefits in force is to use the current salary of the position which the pensioner occupied at the time of retirement as against the salary of that position at that time. Such an approach is only possible in occupations where there is a clear compartmentalization of job categories, such as in military service or among police officers and fire fighters. Thus, for example, a person retiring as a colonel at a certain percentage of final salary would, under this approach, have a pension that would always be that same percentage of the current salary of a colonel.

In essence, this indexing method is really a procedure for indexing by wages, but in this instance by the specific earnings in the particular job classification. Accordingly, it tends to have the same pros and cons as compared with indexing by prices as does indexing by general wage levels.

One particular difficulty with indexing by job classification is that, for reasons unrelated to the pension plan, job classifications might change significantly over the years, the salary levels no longer being consistent. This would be much more likely to occur in civilian employment than in military service. Thus, for example, the various job classifications in federal civilian service have changed drastically over the years, and proper comparability might no longer be present if job classifications were used as a basis for indexing pensions. It would therefore seem that indexing by job classification, except under very unusual circumstances, is not a desirable approach because peculiar or undesirable results might derive for reasons not at all connected with the operation of the pension plan.

INDEXING BY COMBINATION OF METHODS

It would also be possible to have automatic adjustment of pensions in course of payment by using a combination of the foregoing methods or else an alternative of them. For example, the percentage change could be based on the average of the percentage changes of both prices and wages. Another approach would be to use whichever of the two changes is the smaller (or, conversely as another possible procedure, whichever is the larger).

Still another basis would be to have a guaranteed increasing pension (say, at a rate of 3 percent annually) and to have an adjustment on top thereof based on changes in the CPI. Such adjustment might be made by having a further increase equal to the excess of the CPI rise over 3 percent, perhaps with a maximum on the adjustment (such as 2 percent) or perhaps recognizing only a certain proportion of the excess (such as 65 percent). In this way, a sizable proportion of the advance funding needed could be readily recognized and determined.

INDEXING DURING DEFERRED PERIODS

The foregoing discussion has related to indexing of pensions in course of payment. A closely related matter is what procedure should be followed for deferred pensions with respect to individuals who have separated from service with vested rights to a pension at the normal retirement age. Several different procedures are possible.

If the earnings record on which the pension is to be based is indexed for changes in some economic factor (as is now the case for the U.S. social security program—see Chapter 4—or as prevails in some foreign social insurance programs—see Chapters 6 and 7), the result is indexing during the deferred period. The same result obtains in pension plans where the benefit amount is based on the current salary of the particular job classification.

Alternatively, the pension amount may be determined in monetary units at the time of separation from service and indexed thereafter (both before and after attainment of the age when the pension becomes payable) on the basis of some economic factor (as is done for Canadian government employees—see Chapter 6). On the other hand, there may be no indexing of the pension amount determined on the basis of service and salary at the date of separation from service until the pension actually becomes payable; this approach is followed under the U.S. Civil Service Retirement system—see Chapter 5.

When there is no indexing during the deferred period, there is the disadvantage that under the inflationary conditions, the pension ultimately payable may lose much of its value in terms of purchasing power. Thus, an individual with service under different pension plans (even though indexed after the pensions begin) will be not nearly as well off as another person who has the same salary history and length of service but all under one plan, as long as there is no indexing during the deferred period. Quite obviously, it can be very costly to provide such indexing.

FUNDING OF INDEXED PENSIONS

The consideration of indexing of pension benefits in force would not be complete without some reference to the method of funding such provisions. It is beyond the scope of this monograph to go into all the technical aspects of this subject, but a brief discussion seems worthwhile. It will be limited to the funding of private pension plans and public-employee pension plans because the funding for social insurance systems is necessarily on a quite different basis (in most countries, involving current-cost, or pay-as-you-go, financing, regardless of the structure of the benefits).

At one extreme of funding of private and public-employee plans is the pay-as-you-go approach. In general, this does not seem to be an acceptable procedure for the funding of the indexing of the pensions because if the plan were terminated, the pensions would, at best, revert to their original unindexed amounts.

At the other extreme, there could be full funding of possible future indexation that would be accomplished during the time that the employees are in active service. This would necessarily involve the difficult (if not impossible) problem of estimating the inflation rate for many years into the future. At times, the argument has been made in this respect that it is no more difficult to estimate postretirement cost-of-living increases than to estimate the future salary trends to be used in the valuation of a pension plan. Although this may be the case, it is important to note that if salaries are incorrectly estimated, then the resulting error in the pension liabilities will be offset to a considerable extent by the similar error in estimating contribution income, whereas no such offsetting item exists in connection with indexation of pensions.

Thus, under this approach of attempting to fully fund all future indexation of pensions, in the event of termination of the plan, the assets on hand would be *more than sufficient* to pay the accrued pensions on a flat basis. In fact, such assets would be sufficient to provide future indexation for both pensioners and active employees. Most employers would, quite naturally, consider such a reserve to be grossly excessive, and they would argue that future inflation should not be anticipated but rather dealt with when it arises.

A middle course would be to fund only the pension increases (on a life-annuity basis) as the increases are made. This is, of course, somewhat similar to terminal funding, but might well be considered appropriate under the circumstances. If this were done, then in the event of plan termination, no pensions would have to be reduced, but no provision would have been made for future indexation.

Indexing of U.S. Social Security Benefits

The Old-Age, Survivors, and Disability Insurance program in the United States, commonly referred to as "Social Security," provides a basic floor of protection against the risks of loss of income through old-age retirement, long-term disability, and death of the breadwinner.[1] This system applies to virtually the entire work force of the country. The major noncovered groups are the vast majority of the civilian employees of the federal government (who have their own separate retirement system) and a substantial proportion of the employees of state and local governments (who generally also have separate retirement systems).

Railroad workers are covered by a separate federal program, the railroad retirement system. However, as a result of legislation in 1974, in essence, a portion of the railroad retirement benefit can properly be considered as a social security benefit, and its amount is subject to the same automatic-adjustment provisions. Portions of the remainder of the railroad retirement benefit are also automatically adjusted, in some instances by only 65 percent of the increase in the Consumer Price Index.[2] Similarly, individuals eligible for or receiving railroad retirement benefits participate in the Medicare

---

[1] For more details on the Old-Age, Survivors, and Disability Insurance program, see Robert J. Myers, *Social Security* (Homewood, Ill.: Richard D. Irwin, Inc., 1975), pp. 21–82.

[2] For more details, ibid., pp. 466–70.

program in exactly the same manner as do those under social security.

Monthly benefits have been payable under the social security program since 1940. Quite naturally, in order that the program should accomplish its social purposes, the benefit level has been adjusted from time to time in order to keep it up to date with changes in economic conditions. On a few occasions—primarily in the legislation in 1954 and during 1968–72—the real level of the benefits was raised; but at all other times, the changes essentially reflected increases in the general price level. (See Table 1.)

TABLE 1
History of Social Security General Benefit Increase

Month When First Effective	(1) Percentage Benefit Increase*	(2) Increase in CPI from Previous Effective Date	(3) Column (1) Minus Column (2)
September 1950	77%†	75.5%‡	+1.5%
September 1952	15†	9.3	+5.7
September 1954	13†	0.5	+12.5
January 1959	7	7.9	−0.9
January 1965	7	7.9	−0.9
February 1968	13	9.3	+3.7
January 1970	15	10.8	+4.2
January 1971	10	5.2	+4.8
September 1972	20	5.9	+14.1
June 1974	11§	16.4	−5.4
June 1975	8.0‖	9.3	−1.3
June 1976	6.4‖	5.4	+1.0
June 1977	5.9‖	6.9	−1.0
June 1978	6.5‖	6.6**	−0.1

   * All benefit increases, except those for September 1950, 1952, and 1954, were uniform across-the-board increases (at times, although not for 1965 and later, with somewhat larger proportionate increases in the minimum benefit).
   † Average increase in benefits for those then on the roll.
   ‡ Measured from January 1940.
   § Made in two steps, with 7 percent being effective for March 1974.
   ‖ Resulting from automatic-adjustment provisions.
   ** Estimated by the author on basis of actual data through March 1978.

In accordance with the principles of social insurance, benefit increases have been applied more or less equally to those already on the benefit roll and to those qualifying for benefits in the future. This is, of course, in contrast with what might be said to be the individual-equity approach that once persons enter the pension roll, no subsequent benefit increases are justified "because the individual has already bought and paid for his specific benefit."

This chapter will deal not only with the automatic adjustment of benefit amounts but also with the indexing of other benefit features of the social security program. Also considered will be the closely related matter of indexing the earnings record from which benefit amounts are derived.

METHOD OF INCREASING BENEFITS BEFORE 1972

Before 1972, social security benefits in course of payment were increased by ad hoc legislation. Generally, the procedure was to give a uniform percentage increase to all beneficiaries that tended to parallel the change in the cost of living. At the same time, the benefit formula applicable to future claimants was adjusted so that they too would receive the same percentage increase. For example, the "new start" benefit formula in the 1954 Act was 55 percent of the first $110 of Average Monthly Wage (AMW), plus 20 percent of AMW in excess of $110.[3] When the 1958 Act increased the general benefit level by 7 percent, the benefit formula became 58.85 percent of the first $110 of AMW, plus 21.4 percent of AMW in excess of $110. In other words, each of the benefit factors of the 1954 formula were multiplied by 1.07.

This same general procedure was followed when subsequent legislation provided further percentage increases in the general benefit level so that the benefit formula as it stood in January 1978 (following the application of the automatic-adjustment procedures, described hereafter, which followed the same processes as the ad hoc changes in 1972 and earlier) was in the following complex form:

145.90 percent of the first $110 of AMW, plus 53.07 percent of the next $290,

plus 49.59 percent of the next $150, plus 58.29 percent of the next $100,

plus 32.42 percent of the next $100, plus 27.02 percent of the next $250,

plus 24.34 percent of the next $175, plus 22.54 percent of the next $100,

---

[3] The Average Monthly Wage is, in essence, a career average, measured over the period after 1950 and up to the minimum retirement age, with the lowest five years of earnings being omitted and with any years of high earnings before age 22 and at or after such retirement age being substituted for years of low earnings in such period. The "old start" benefit formula utilizes earnings back to 1937 and is currently used by relatively few persons currently claiming benefits because it produces smaller amounts than the "new start" method.

plus 21.28 percent of the next $100, plus 20.00 percent of the next $100,

with the minimum benefit being $114.30.

It may be noted that the various additional steps resulted from the periodic increases in the maximum creditable earnings from the $3,600 applicable in 1951–54 to the $17,700 applicable in 1978.

GENERAL METHOD OF INCREASING BENEFITS AFTER 1972

In 1972, legislation was enacted that provided for automatic adjustment of social security benefits in course of payment. The procedure that would be followed would be exactly the same as had been done under the various ad hoc changes in the past. The same percentage increase would apply for benefits in course of payment and for the percentage factors in the benefit formula. A 20 percent factor would apply to any increase in the maximum creditable earnings base.

The first automatic adjustment was to take place for the January 1975 benefits, on the basis of the percentage change in the Consumer Price Index (CPI), prepared by the Bureau of Labor Statistics of the U.S. Department of Labor, from the third quarter of 1972 (when the 20 percent benefit increase under the 1972 Act first became effective) to the second quarter of 1974. All subsequent automatic adjustments of benefits were to be effective for January benefits, being based on the percentage increase in the CPI from the second quarter of the second preceding year to the second quarter of the preceding year (such second quarters are referred to as "base quarters").[4]

---

[4] The CPI is expressed in relation to an index of 100 for the CPI base period (in recent years, the average CPI for 1967) and is given to one decimal place (for example, being 170.1 for June 1976). The CPI for a quarter is merely the average for the three months involved, rounded to one decimal place. For example, for the first quarter of 1975, the three CPIs were 156.1, 157.2, and 157.8, so that the average was 157.0 ⅓, which was rounded to 157.0. The law specifies that the CPI unadjusted for seasonal variation (which is the basis most commonly quoted) is to be used. As discussed in Chapter 3, three alternative CPIs are being published in 1978. That based on the definition and concept used in the past was utilized for the computation of the June 1978 increase, while that for all urban consumers will, under a proposal sponsored by the Carter Administration, be used for subsequent determinations (June 1979 and after). Rather surprisingly (and inconsistently), the CPI used for the first quarter of 1978 was that based on the broader sample of items included in one of the two new CPIs (see page 19), while that for the first quarter of 1977 was based on a different, smaller sample (i.e., the numerator and denominator were from different series). The resulting actual benefit increase of 6.5 percent would, instead, have been only 6.4 percent if a consistent comparison had been made. It is interesting to note that this difference will result in additional outgo over future years of about $1 billion.

A "trigger" of at least a 3 percent increase in the CPI is required in order that the resulting increase in benefits would justify the great amount of administrative work involved.[5] When such an increase occurs, the base quarter is called a "cost-of-living computation quarter." If the increase is not as much as 3 percent, then no benefit increase would occur, and the computation base quarter would remain the same for the next year's determination. For example, if the CPI had increased only 2 percent from the second quarter of 1977 to the second quarter of 1978, there would be no automatic benefit increase for January 1979. Then, the determination as to the benefit increase for January 1980 would be based on the change in the CPI from the second quarter of 1977 to the second quarter of 1979.

It will be observed that as legislated, the automatics can only increase benefits, never decrease them. In all logic, the procedure should work both ways, and if the CPI declines by 3 percent or more, benefits should be adjusted correspondingly. Probably, the principal reason that this procedure was not included was political—namely, the undesirability of reducing social security benefits and thereby unleashing complaints from the constituents concerned.

Also, as a practical matter, in the past few decades, the CPI has rarely decreased significantly, and even then it rose to its former level fairly soon. Looking at annual data in this century, there have been the following instances when decreases occurred:

1. From 1901 to 1902, a decrease of 2.8 percent, which was more than offset in 1903.
2. From 1903 to 1904, a decrease of 1.1 percent, which was more than offset by 1906.
3. From 1907 to 1908, a decrease of 4.3 percent, which also held for 1909, but was more than offset in 1910.
4. From 1912 to 1913, a decrease of 1.9 percent, which was almost completely offset in 1914.
5. From 1920 to 1921, a decrease of 10.7 percent, followed by a further decrease of 6.3 percent from 1921 to 1922; the 1920 level was not reached again until 1947.

---

[5] The percentage increase is rounded to the nearest 0.1 percent. For example, as to the increase effective for June 1976, the ratio of the CPI for the first quarter of 1976 (167.1) to that for the first quarter of 1975 (157.0) was 1.06433 (as will be discussed subsequently, legislation in 1973 changed the basis for base quarters from second quarters to first ones). As a result, the increase was 6.4 percent.

6. From 1926 to 1927, a decrease of 1.8 percent, followed by small decreases each year to 1930, which was 5.5 percent below 1926.
7. From 1930 to 1933, sizable decreases each year, aggregating 22.5 percent.
8. From 1937 to 1939, decreases each year, aggregating 3.2 percent, which was more than offset in 1941.
9. From 1948 to 1949, a decrease of 1.0 percent, which was offset in 1950.
10. From 1954 to 1955, a decrease of 0.3 percent, which was more than offset in 1956.

With the exception of the decreases in 1920–22 and 1926–33, no periods had declines of such an order that a "decrease" provision under the automatics would have been very significant. It could be argued that the unusual economic conditions which arose following World War I and again during the Great Depression will never occur again so that a "decrease" provision is not needed. On the other hand, if for some reason now unforeseeable, the CPI should drop drastically at some time in the future, Congress could reduce benefits by ad hoc action. Certainly, this would be justified; at the same time, it is almost certain that the earnings of the working population, who are paying the payroll taxes to provide the social security benefits, would be sharply lower.

No legal contract exists with regard to any aspects of the social security program, only statutory rights. As a result, Congress can change any provisions as it so desires (as long as no discriminatory treatment of any individual or groups occurs). Accordingly, the 1972 Act provided that the automatic-adjustment provisions would not be applicable if ad hoc benefit increases were either legislated or would become effective in the year before the particular January to which an automatic increase would otherwise apply.

Before the automatic-adjustment provisions became operative, they were changed by congressional action at the end of 1973. The underlying reason for this legislation was the rapid price inflation which occurred following the previous legislation in 1972. As a result, many persons believed that a benefit increase was called for well before the January 1975 initial date for the automatic increases.

Accordingly, the 1973 Act provided an 11 percent benefit increase, effective for June 1974 (with an interim temporary smaller increase, 7 percent, for March to May 1974).

At the same time, the 1973 Act revised the automatic-adjustment provisions by making them first applicable for June 1975, rather than January 1975, and then for subsequent Junes, instead of Januaries. The percentage increase in benefits for June 1975 was based on the change in the CPI from the second quarter of 1974 (when the ad hoc 11 percent benefit increase under these amendments first became effective) to the first quarter of 1975. On an ongoing basis, the measurement of the change in the CPI is as between base quarters which are first quarters.

As under the 1972 Act, the revised procedure developing from the 1973 Act provided for the suspension of any automatic benefit increase whenever Congress legislated ad hoc increases, either enacted in the year prior to the year in which the automatic increase would occur or becoming effective in that year. It could happen that such a procedure would produce less favorable benefit results for the beneficiaries. The ad hoc legislation could provide a smaller increase than the automatic adjustment would have done. Or else two automatic adjustments could be suspended because of one piece of legislation; for example, a law enacted in January 1978 which provided for a benefit increase for January 1979 would eliminate the automatic adjustments for both June 1978 and June 1979. It seems unlikely, however, in the real political world that this would occur; Congress could always pass legislation to do otherwise.

The legislation also contains provisions for advance notice to Congress that an automatic increase in benefits seems imminent. The law provides that the Secretary of Health, Education, and Welfare shall notify the House Committee on Ways and Means and the Senate Committee on Finance (the two congressional committees with responsibility for social security) by April 30 if an automatic benefit increase will occur for the coming June, and the amount of such increase. Actually, the amount of the increase is known after April 30, since this is when the CPI for March (the third month of the first quarter) is released. The Secretary is also required to publish the amount of the benefit increase in the *Federal Register* by May 15.

The aforementioned report to the two congressional committees is also supposed to contain an actuarial estimate of the extent to which, over the long range, the cost of the automatic benefit increase will be met by the increase in the maximum taxable earnings base triggered thereby (effective the following January)—as will be discussed subsequently. Such report is also supposed to include a statement of the actuarial assumptions and methodology underlying such estimate. This provision will be impossible to implement in the future because the extent of the increase in the earnings base will not be known by the preceding April 30 (originally, the promulgation of these elements was made near the end of the year, so such analysis could be made). Furthermore, such analysis does not portray the full story; much of the cost of the benefit increase is met by the higher general earnings level likely when prices rise (considering also the effect of the weighted benefit formula).

The law also calls for another report from the Secretary of Health, Education, and Welfare to the congressional committees to give advance notice of the possibility of the automatics going into operation. Such report is to be made whenever the CPI for a particular month is at least 2.5 percent higher than the CPI for the most recent computation quarter (and is to be given within five days of the publication of the CPI for such month). For example, such a report was made for July 1975, when the CPI was 162.3, or 3.4 percent higher than the CPI for the first quarter of 1975 (157.0); the corresponding figure for June 1975 was 2.3 percent.

Quite evidently, the purpose of these reports is to give Congress a chance to take action of its own through ad hoc increases. No attempt of any significance was made to do this before the first four automatic increases, for June of 1975, 1976, 1977, and 1978.

When Congress enacts an ad hoc benefit increase, the base quarter from which measurement is made for the next computation quarter under the automatic-adjustment provisions is the quarter for which such ad hoc increase is effective. For example, if legislation were enacted in August 1980 increasing benefits effective for October 1980 (after an automatic increase had already occurred for June 1980), the next automatic increase possible would be for June 1982. Such increase would be based on the change in the CPI from the fourth quarter of 1980 to the first quarter of 1982.

It could be argued that the base quarter determined with regard to an ad hoc increase should be the quarter before the quarter in which such increase first becomes effective, instead of being such quarter. Such basis would be consistent with the procedure under the automatics, where the base quarters are the first quarters, as against the benefit increases being effective in second quarters. On the other hand, this approach could be considered as some offset for the ad hoc increases almost certainly being larger than what would have resulted under the automatics.

Such an effect of a smaller benefit increase under the automatics after an ad hoc increase had occurred took place in the increase for June 1975. The increase was measured over only a nine-month period (the second quarter of 1974 to the first quarter of 1975) and was 8.0 percent. If the increase had been determined on a 12-month basis, as between first quarters, it would have been 11.0 percent.

EFFECT OF AD HOC BENEFIT INCREASE IN 1974

As Table 1 shows, the ad hoc benefit increase effective for June 1974 was inadequate by about 5 percent if its purpose was to keep the benefit level up to date with changes in the CPI after the last previous benefit increase. On the other hand, it could well be argued that the previous benefit increase had been excessive (by about 14 percent), and so this deficiency in the 1974 increase was merely a partial correction of the situation. Or it could be argued that the benefit increase in the 1972 Act was intentionally larger than "necessary" so as to compensate in advance for some of the inflation expected in the next few months.

Still another item of interest is whether the ad hoc benefit increase under the 1973 Act, combined with the deferment of five months in the automatic-adjustment provisions resulting therefrom, was of long-run value to the beneficiaries, or, in other words, represented a real benefit liberalization. Table 2 presents such an analysis for individuals on the roll in February 1974.

A hypothetical Primary Insurance Amount (PIA) of $200 has been used (although the same general results would be shown for any other PIA). Comparison is made of the actual experience for such individual, beginning with March 1974, as against what would have been payable under the original basis of the automatic-adjustment provisions if they had not been changed and if there had been no ad hoc benefit increase in 1974.

Quite naturally, the actual experience resulted in more benefits being payable under the actual experience during 1974. But then during the first five months of 1975, the initial basis would have

TABLE 2
Situation if 1972 Automatic-Adjustment Provisions Had Remained in Effect,
Considering a Case of a Hypothetical PIA of $200 for February 1974

Period	Actual Experience	Payable under 1972 Act	Cumulative Excess of Actual Payments over 1972 Act*
March–May 1974	$214.00	$200.00	$ 42.00
June–December 1974	222.00	200.00	196.00
January–May 1975	222.00	233.20†	140.00
June–December 1975	239.80‡	233.20	186.20
January–May 1976	239.80	255.90†	105.70
June–December 1976	255.20‡	255.90	100.80
January–May 1977	255.20	271.60†	18.80
June–December 1977	270.30‡	271.60	9.70
January–May 1978	270.30	290.10†	−89.30
June–December 1978	287.90	290.10	− 104.70

* As of end of period shown.
† These increases would have been 16.6 percent, 9.7 percent, 6.1 percent, and 6.8 percent, respectively, under the provisions of the 1972 Act.
‡ Based on the actual increases of 8.0 percent, 6.4 percent, 5.9 percent, and 6.5 percent, respectively.

provided larger benefits because the automatics would have come into operation five months earlier. The relative situation then shifted back and forth. This will continue to occur in the future.

As it turns out, almost exactly the same benefit is payable in the last seven months of 1976, 1977, and 1978 under either the actual experience or that which would have occurred under the original provisions.

The last column of the table compares the cumulative excess of the payments actually made with those which would have occurred under the original basis of the automatic-adjustment provisions and without the ad hoc benefit increase which was enacted for 1974. The actual cumulative payments were significantly in excess of those that would have occurred under the original basis in the 1972 Amendments through 1976—by almost as much as one month's benefit at times. However, beginning in 1976, this cumulative excess began to decline, and as of the end of the year it was only about $101.

Then, as of the end of 1977, this cumulative excess was almost eliminated. In other words, about the same overall effect occurred, despite the change in the automatic-adjustment provisions and the ad hoc benefit increase in 1974. In fact, after 1977, the situation reverses, and the overall effect will be less favorable under present law than it would have been if the changes made in the 1974 Amendments had not occurred. This thus indicates that the ad hoc benefit increases made in the 1973 legislation were not really an abrogation or overriding of the principles of the automatic-adjustment provisions enacted in 1972, but rather were merely an approximately equivalent advancing of the date of the first increase.

DETAILS OF INCREASING BENEFITS UNDER AUTOMATICS PRIOR TO 1977 AMENDMENTS

Let us now examine in more detail how the automatics operate to increase social security benefits once the percentage increase factor has been determined.

Previously, reference has been made to the benefit formula that was applicable to the benefit computations for new retirees (old age and disability) and for survivor beneficiaries newly created as the law was before the 1977 Amendments. Actually, the law contained a benefit table giving the primary benefit (the amount payable to a worker retiring at age 65 or to a disabled worker) and the maximum family benefit for each AMW. Such table was derived, as to the primary benefit, from the benefit formula (with small differences, due primarily to rounding). The maximum family benefits were varying multiples of the primary benefit.[6] The provisions of the law relating to the automatic adjustments describe precisely how this table was to be revised and extended from time to time to reflect the resulting percentage benefit increases and the increases in the maximum taxable (and thus creditable) earnings base.

First, considering persons on the benefit roll at the time, the percentage increase was, with two exceptions noted later, applied directly to each of the various benefits payable to persons in the beneficiary family, and the result was, if not an exact multiple of 10 cents, rounded up to the next dime. For example, a benefit to a

---

[6] The maximum family benefit was 150 percent of the primary benefit for AMWs of less than $240. This proportion increased thereafter until it reached 188 percent for an AMW of $432–436. Then, for higher AMWs, it decreased until leveling off at 175 percent for AMWs of $628 and above. This rather peculiar relationship developed, in large part, by historical accident.

worker who retired at age 65 was $205.10 payable for May 1976 was raised to $218.30 for June 1976 as a result of the 6.4 percent benefit increase (6.4 percent of $205.10 is $218.23).[7] The result for the total of the family's benefits is that it was also increased by the percentage increase, plus perhaps a small additional amount due to the rounding upward of each of the individual benefits.[8] This procedure is continued under the 1977 Amendments.

The new benefit table, similarly, was obtained by increasing each of the primary benefits and maximum family benefits by the percentage-increase factor and rounding the result up to the next dime, if rounding was necessary. It should be noted that the maximum family benefit can be exceeded by the sum of the individual benefits to which it applied if this occurred because of the rounding to dimes.

The first exception to this procedure of increasing benefits for those on the roll applied to the relatively small category of workers receiving the special minimum benefit of $9 per year of coverage[9] in excess of 10, but not in excess of 30 (only 400 such cases in July 1977). The law specifically excluded this particular category from the operations of the automatics. Congress took this action knowingly so that the special-minimum provision would phase out (because the regular minimum benefit was indexed and thus gradually had more and more effect as compared with the special minimum), and it was not an oversight; the logic of such procedure was, in the author's view, questionable. This procedure was changed by the 1977 Amendments, and these benefits will be updated in January 1979 to what they would have been if they had been subject to automatic adjustment (namely, to $11.50 per year of coverage),

---

[7] A rather peculiar rounding rule was followed which arose from regulations rather than the law or congressional intent as expressed in committee reports or floor debate. If the unrounded product was at all larger than the exact 10 cents figure, the result is rounded up to the next dime. For example, the May 1975 primary benefit of $203.20 when increased by 6.4 percent yielded $216.2048; under customary rounding procedures, this would be taken as $216.20 and left at that figure, but actually it was raised to $216.30.

[8] The maximum family benefit applies to all benefits payable on a single earnings record except those for a divorced spouse (such as wife, widow, or widowed mother). A special rule applies to survivor children eligible on the earnings records of both parents.

[9] Defined, in general, as a year in which credited earnings were at least equal to 25 percent of the maximum taxable earnings base (but for 1937–50, the years of coverage are total wages in such period divided by $900, rounded down to the nearest integer but not to exceed 14 in any case). Under the 1977 Amendments (which injected sharp ad hoc increases in the earnings base in 1979–81), the earnings bases to be used for determining years of coverage are those which would have occurred under the previous law.

and they will be subject to automatic adjustment for increases in the CPI.

The second exception to the straightforward procedure of increasing benefits occurred for persons who received so-called actuarially reduced benefits because of first claiming them before a specified age. Specifically, such reductions apply for old-age retirement benefits claimed first at ages 62–64 (reduction at a rate of 6⅔ percent per year); wife's or husband's benefits when no eligible child is present claimed first at ages 62–64 (reduction of 8⅓ percent per year); widow's or widower's benefits claimed first at ages 60–64 (reduction of 5.7 percent per year); and disabled widow's or widower's benefits claimed first at ages 50–59 (reduction of 28½ percent, plus 2.15 percent per year below age 60). Actually, only the reduction factor for retired workers is ''actuarial'' in the sense that, on the average, no additional cost is involved for the social security system if individuals claim benefits early. In other words, the reduction factors for spouses and widows and widowers are less than actuarially necessary to prevent the program from having additional cost.[10]

The procedure which was followed when a percentage benefit increase occurs was to apply it to the unreduced benefit and then to reduce the resulting figure by the reduction factor at the *then-attained* age, not the factor for the initial age at claim. For example, consider a retired worker whose primary benefit was $200 when benefits were first claimed at age 62 and who thus received a reduced benefit of $160 (i.e., a 20 percent reduction rate). If a 10 percent benefit increase occurred after 1½ years, the worker's new benefit rate was $178 ($160, plus 90 percent of 10 percent of $200). The increase was based on a 10 percent reduction factor because the attained age then was 63½ and was 11¼ percent higher than the original rate of $160. The new primary-benefit rate was $220. Likewise, if a 5 percent benefit increase occurred after another 18 months, the new benefit rate was $189 ($178, plus 5 percent of $220). Any increase arising after the worker attained age 65 was payable at the full rate of the increase applied to the primary benefit amount as increased previously.

This complex procedure for increasing benefits in cases where

---

[10] The reduction factor for spouse's benefits, despite being larger than the factor for retired workers, is actually too low because it is applicable during the period of the joint lifetime of the couple (which is shorter than the lifetime of one person alone).

early claim was made was readily handled administratively through electronic data processing equipment. It was, however, difficult for beneficiaries to understand why, in some cases, larger relative increases were paid than the announced general increase. Such lack of understanding was not too serious from a public relations viewpoint because the actual increase was always *larger* than the publicized one, and accordingly nobody was ever disappointed. The general rationale for this procedure was that the same increase in terms of dollars should be given whether or not the individual had claimed benefits early.

However, this rationale can be questioned from a technical standpoint.[11] It can be shown mathematically that under stable economic conditions, with interest rates close to the "real" interest rate of 3 percent under noninflationary conditions, this procedure was proper when there were ad hoc increases raising the "real" level of social security benefits relative to wages and prices. On the other hand, when benefits were increased solely due to price changes (which also had an effect on interest rates), the procedure was wrong. Instead, the percentage benefit increase should merely have been applied to the *reduced* benefit actually being paid. That would, of course, have resulted in a smaller benefit increase in some cases (but uniform for all benefits).

In support of this view, it can be argued that with regard to retired workers, the actuarial-equivalent reduction factors are based on an interest rate consistent with noninflationary conditions. In comparison with the actual 20 percent factor for retirement at age 62, we may consider the theoretical factor based on the 1955 American Annuity Table[12] at 3 percent interest. The resulting factors are 18.4 percent for females and 21.1 percent for males. On the basis of these factors, the 80 percent factor used in the social security system seemed a reasonable, simple approximation.

If, however, there are inflationary conditions, and if interest rates are higher than the "real" or "true" rate of 3 percent, the

---

[11] Acknowledgment is made of research done in this area by Steven F. McKay, F.S.A., Office of the Actuary, Social Security Administration.

[12] This table is used here because the date of this table was approximately when the provisions of the law being discussed were adopted and because this table, being based on annuitant mortality, makes some allowance for possible future improvement in the mortality of social security beneficiaries.

reduction factors for early retirement would be higher if they are determined from a higher interest rate. For example, using 5 percent interest with the 1955 American Annuity Table, the female factor is 21.9 percent and the male factor is 24.5 percent, or an average of 23.2 percent, as compared with the 20 percent in the law.

Thus, because the reduction factors in the law are based on the assumption of noninflationary conditions, it could be argued that any percentage benefit increases due solely to cost-of-living changes should be applied directly to the actual reduced benefit payable, rather than the previous procedure. If the previous procedure had been retained, then by this same logic, the reduction factors should have been determined on the basis of higher interest rates as reflective of inflationary conditions. For this reason, the procedure was changed by the 1977 Amendments so that the percentage benefit increase will always be applied to the actual reduced benefit payable.

INDEXING OF EARNINGS RECORDS UNDER 1977 AMENDMENTS

The 1977 Amendments provided for so-called decoupling of the benefit computation for new claimants from that applicable to beneficiaries on the roll whenever automatic adjustments to recognize increases in the CPI or ad hoc increases are made.[13] The basic principle underlying the change is to index the earnings record and then to calculate the Average Indexed Monthly Earnings (AIME) and apply it to a new benefit formula. This new procedure is applicable only for persons attaining age 62, becoming disabled, or dying after 1978. For all other persons, the procedure of previous law is continued, as though the 1977 Amendments had not been enacted.

The earnings record is indexed to the *second* year before attainment of age 62, or before becoming disabled or dying before age

---

[13] For an excellent account of the underlying reasons for and principles of decoupling, see E. J. Moorhead and C. L. Trowbridge, "The Unresolved OASDI Decoupling Issue," *Transactions,* Society of Actuaries, vol. 24, 1977 (and the discussion thereof by Robert J. Myers).

62.[14] The two-year lag is necessary because the data to be used for indexing are not available for any later date. The AIME is then calculated from the indexed earnings record in exactly the same manner as the AMW was under previous law, that is, on a career-average basis from 1951 on (or, if later, from age 22 on), with a dropout of the five lowest years). Table 3 shows data on past average wages which might be used for indexing earnings in the period 1951–77 to 1977, which will be the base indexing year for the 1979 beneficiary cohort. Also shown as a matter of possible interest are corresponding CPI data.

INITIAL COMPUTATION OF BENEFITS UNDER 1977 AMENDMENTS

A new benefit formula for the PIA is applicable to the AIME, with a different one for each annual cohort of attainments of age 62, or prior disability or death. The formula for the 1979 cohort is: 90 percent of the first $180 of AIME, plus 32 percent of the next $905 of AIME, plus 15 percent of AIME in excess of $1,085, with a minimum benefit of $122,[15] rounded to the next higher $0.10 if not an even multiple of $0.10. For future cohorts, this formula will be modified by changing the dollar figures; they will be multiplied by the ratio of the average wage for the country for the second year preceding the cohort's year to the average for 1977 (and rounding to the nearest dollar), but with no change in the amount of the minimum benefit.

Persons attaining age 62 in 1979–83 can, if a higher PIA results,

---

[14] Indexing, which in essence means expressing the past actual earnings in "real" terms relative to the wage level of the year to which indexing is done, is accomplished on the basis of the average of total wages in all employment in the country (not merely in covered employment, and without regard to the maximum taxable earnings base) in various previous years. Such data for 1977 and after will be obtained from income tax returns, while for earlier years (back through 1951) the Secretary of Health, Education, and Welfare will, by regulation, develop the appropriate figures. Indexing of the actual recorded earnings for a particular year is done by multiplying such earnings by the ratio of (1) the average wage for the year to which indexing is being done to (2) the average wage for the particular year. For example, if actual covered earnings in 1960 were $4,000, and if the average wage in the year to which the earnings record is being indexed is twice that for 1960, then the indexed earnings for 1960 are taken as $8,000. The earnings for the year to which indexing is being done and for all subsequent years (including years after age 62 for those who retire or die thereafter) are used in their actual amounts.

[15] This figure is that which will be the minimum PIA in the benefit table under previous law in June 1978 (after the automatic adjustment occurring then), rounded up to the next higher dollar.

TABLE 3
Possible Data to Be Used for Indexing Earnings Record to 1977 and
Data on Consumer Price Index, 1951–1977

Year	First-Quarter Average Wage*			Consumer Price Index†		
	Amount	Increase	Factor‡	Amount	Increase	Factor
1951	$2,769	—	3.532	77.8	—	2.333
1952	2,945	6.4%	3.321	79.5	2.2%	2.283
1953	3,089	4.9	3.166	80.1	0.8	2.266
1954	3,226	4.4	3.031	80.5	0.5	2.255
1955	3,350	3.8	2.919	80.2	−0.4	2.263
1956	3,540	5.7	2.763	81.4	1.5	2.230
1957	3,747	5.8	2.610	84.3	3.6	2.153
1958	3,852	2.8	2.539	86.6	2.7	2.096
1959	3,980	3.3	2.457	87.3	0.8	2.079
1960	4,148	4.2	2.358	88.7	1.6	2.046
1961	4,283	3.3	2.283	89.6	1.0	2.026
1962	4,461	4.2	2.192	90.6	1.1	2.003
1963	4,572	2.5	2.139	91.7	1.2	1.979
1964	4,712	3.1	2.075	92.9	1.3	1.954
1965	4,787	1.6	2.043	94.5	1.7	1.921
1966	4,997	4.4	1.957	97.2	2.9	1.867
1967	5,311	6.3	1.841	100.0	2.9	1.815
1968	5,683	7.0	1.721	104.2	4.2	1.742
1969	5,977	5.2	1.636	109.8	5.4	1.653
1970	6,288	5.2	1.555	116.3	5.9	1.561
1971	6,670	6.1	1.466	121.3	4.3	1.496
1972 ......:.	7,250	8.7	1.349	125.3	3.3	1.449
1973	7,580	4.6	1.290	133.1	6.2	1.364
1974	8,031	5.9	1.218	147.7	11.0	1.229
1975	8,631	7.5	1.133	161.2	9.1	1.126
1976	9,226	6.9	1.060	170.5	5.8	1.065
1977	9,779§	6.0§	1.000	181.5	6.5	1.000

* Annualized average taxable earnings for all persons with covered nonagricultural wages in first quarter of year (data furnished by Social Security Administration).

† All figures based on 1967 equaling 100 (data from various issues of *Social Security Bulletin*).

‡ If this series were used for indexing the earnings record, the factor for a particular year would be multipled by the individual's earnings recorded for that year to yield indexed earnings as indexed to 1977.

§ This figure was unusually low because of the low level of economic activity in the first quarter of 1977 due to the abnormally cold weather and the accompanying energy-shortages problems. Based on the general trend of wages in 1977 as a whole, the average wage would have been about $9,870–$9,960, an increase of 7–8 percent over 1976.

use a modified version of the AMW method of previous law, but with significant limitations, so that generally it will be applicable only to the 1979 and 1980 cohorts. The PIA formula set forth on page 27, as adjusted to June 1978 (by increasing each of the percentage factors by the benefit increase in that month—which was 6.5 percent), will be frozen thereafter. Further, the AMW will be computed *exclusive* of any covered earnings in the year of attaining age 62 and in subsequent years.

Persons who attained age 21 after 1936[16] and who had credited wages before 1951 can use an "old start" benefit formula for the PIA if this produces a higher amount. This formula is based on the AMW concept, going back to 1937 and using unindexed earnings, with exactly the same procedure as under previous law continued as though the 1977 Amendments had not been enacted (except for technical simplifications as to how wages in 1937–50 are to be allocated to individual years in that period and as to the benefit formula used).

The maximums on total family benefits (MFB) as initially awarded are determined from the PIA by a formula that closely approximates the results under the procedures in previous law as to the relationship of the MFB to the PIA. The MFB formula for each cohort of attainments of age 62 (or prior disability or death) is expressed in several steps of PIA amounts with different percentages being applicable.[17] These dollar steps are varied for different cohorts in exactly the same manner as is done for the PIA formula.

The "special minimum PIA" provision for those with long coverage at low earnings was, in essence, reactivated by increasing the benefit amount per year of coverage in excess of 10 years and not in excess of 30 years from $9 to $11.50, effective in January 1979. This increase brings the benefit amount up to what it would have been if the $9 had been subject to automatic adjustment according to increases in the CPI subsequent to when it was first effective (March 1974). This will make an estimated additional 220,000 persons eligible for increased benefits. It is interesting to note that the definition of "year of coverage" for the future is based on having earnings of 25 percent of the maximum taxable earnings bases which would have resulted under previous law, and not on the higher bases resulting from the ad hoc increases of the 1977 Amendments.

---

[16] Persons who attained age 21 in 1936 or before became age 62 at least by 1977 and therefore have their benefits computed under the provisions of previous law.

[17] The formula for the 1979 cohort is: 150 percent of the first $230 of PIA, plus 272 percent of the next $102 of PIA, plus 134 percent of the next $101 of PIA, plus 175 percent of the PIA in excess of $433, rounded to the next higher $0.10 if not an even multiple of $0.10.

DETAILS OF INCREASING BENEFITS UNDER AUTOMATICS UNDER 1977 AMENDMENTS

Although the 1977 Amendments made drastic changes in the method of computing initial benefit amounts, they did not do so for the automatic adjustments of benefits in course of payment (including the maximum-family-benefit provision). The only changes were that the benefits payable under the "special minimum PIA" provision for those with long coverage at low earnings will be subject to automatic adjustment (effective in 1979) and that automatic increases for those with reduced benefits because of retirement before age 65 (or, in the case of spouse's, widow's, and widower's benefits, payment of benefits before age 65) will be based on the amount currently payable, not on the unreduced, full amount.

The Senate version of the 1977 Amendments provided for semiannual automatic adjustments whenever the CPI increased by at least 4 percent in the six months following the base month (changed from the first quarters of calendar years to Februaries and Augusts). If such increase did not occur, the previous 3 percent annual basis would have continued to have been applicable. Such a procedure would have yielded somewhat greater equity to the beneficiaries in that the purchasing power of their benefits would have been better kept up to date in times of great inflation. It could, however, have increased administrative work and resulted in slightly higher benefits costs. However, this provision was dropped by the joint conference committee between the House and the Senate.

METHOD OF INCREASING EARNINGS BASE AND EARNINGS TEST

One element in the computation of social security benefits is the maximum taxable earnings base, which began at $3,000 in 1937–50 and was $16,500 in 1977 and is $17,700 in 1978. This base serves not only as a limit on which the taxes are to be paid each year[18] but also on which benefits are to be computed.

---

[18] The employer pays taxes on up to this maximum for each employee each year and similarly deducts taxes from the employee's pay on this basis. If the employee works for more than one employer in the course of a year and earns a total of more than the maximum, in essence the employee pays taxes on only the maximum because any excess is refundable when income tax is filed. The self-employed person pays taxes on only self-employment income up to the excess of the maximum over any wages earned in the year.

Before the 1972 Act became effective (for 1975 initially), the earnings base had been periodically increased by ad hoc legislation. The 1972 legislation provided for automatic adjustment of the base for 1975 and thereafter on the basis of changes in wages—as against benefits being adjusted on the basis of changes in the CPI. Such different treatment seems reasonable, so that both elements keep up to date with a relevant economic factor.

The specific adjustment procedure for the earnings base initially was based on the percentage change in average taxable wages as between the first quarter of the second year proceeding the year in question and the first quarter of the immediately preceding year. First-quarter taxable wages were used because they are indicative of total wages in covered employment and because they are only affected by the maximum taxable earnings base in the case of workers who earn at an annual rate in excess of four times the base. Such percentage change (only if an increase) was applied to the current year base, and the result was rounded to the nearest $300. It is important to note that the data used for the adjustment were on a 100 percent basis from the pertinent earnings records, not a sample basis (as, for example, is the procedure for developing the CPI).

An increase in the base was made, however, only if it was triggered by an increase in the benefits as a result of the operations of the automatics. In other words, if the CPI did not increase by at least 3 percent between the base period in one year and that in the next year, the earnings base was not increased, no matter how much average earnings had risen. Similarly, if the operation of the automatics was suspended because of an ad hoc benefit increase, the earnings base too would not be automatically adjusted. But, under such circumstances, it would be most likely that the ad hoc legislation also dealt with the base.

Under the initial basis of the automatic adjustment of the benefits being made for Januaries and promulgated on or before the preceding November 1, the earnings base was also adjusted beginning with that January. The necessary first-quarter wage data were readily available, on a virtually full-count basis, by the prescribed date of November 1 in order to make the announcement for the coming year. Self-employment income data were not used because they were reported only annually; the relatively small amount of wage data for farm workers was also not included because reporting for this category was also only on an annual basis.

When the basis of automatically adjusting benefits was changed by the 1973 Act to be applicable for Junes instead of Januaries, the trigger basis for adjusting the earnings base was appropriately modified. An automatic adjustment of benefits for a June was essential to make operative the automatics as to the earnings base for the next year. The ad hoc benefit increase in 1974 was deemed, by a provision in the 1973 Act, to trigger the automatics as to an increase in the earnings base for 1975, and they first came into play then.

Legislation in early 1976, supplemented by the 1977 Amendments, changed the reporting of wages (except for state and local governments and for employers of domestic workers) from a quarterly to an annual basis, effective for 1978. Under such annual reporting, both taxable wages and total wages (i.e., including amounts above the earnings base) must be reported. Accordingly, since first-quarter data would no longer be available, a change in the automatics as they relate to the earnings base was necessary. Moreover, with annual reporting, the data for a year would not be available until some time well after the end of the year and so could not be utilized in determining the base for the next year. Accordingly, an additional year of lag had to be introduced.

The eventual procedure in determining the base for a particular year (assuming that the trigger had gone off) is to use the increase in the average total wage in all employment in the country, not merely in covered employment (without regard to the effect of the maximum taxable earnings base), for the second preceding year over that for the third preceding year. For example, the base for 1981 will be the base for 1980 increased by the increase in average wages from 1978 to 1979. Note that the covered wages of farm workers and wages in noncovered employment will now be used, but not self-employment income (because it is reportable with even more lag than wages—not until April 15 of the next year in most instances).

A transition was required in changing from the quarterly basis to the annual basis in measuring the increase in average wage used to adjust the earnings base. The 1976 Act provided that the quarterly basis would be used in determining the base for 1977–79, but that the basis of a two-year lag would become effective for 1977. In other words, the increase in the base for 1977 (triggered by the 6.4 percent benefit increase that was effective for June 1976) was based on the increase in first-quarter average taxable wages as between 1974 and 1975, which increase had been used for determining the base for 1976. The base for 1978 was determined from the 6.90 percent increase in first-quarter average taxable wages between 1975 and 1976. That for 1979 would have been based on the increase in first-quarter average taxable wages from 1976 to 1977, an increase of 5.99 percent, which would have yielded a base of $18,900, but this was superceded by the ad hoc increase to $22,900 as a result of the 1977 Amendments.

The earnings test under the social security program (frequently called the "retirement test") provides for withholding of benefits for all beneficiaries, except those aged 72 or over (age 70 or over after 1981) or disabled, when substantial work (whether or not in covered employment) is performed.[19] This text operates by exempting annual earnings up to a specified amount and then deducting $1 of benefits for each $2 of excess earnings, but with the proviso that for the initial year of benefit receipt, no benefits are withheld for any month in which wages do not exceed $1/12$ of the annual exempt amount and the individual does not have "substantial services" in self-employment.[20]

The annual exempt amount was established by law at $2,400 for 1974 and is thereafter to be automatically adjusted in the same manner as the maximum taxable earnings base. The only difference is, quite naturally, in connection with the rounding to be done. For the earnings test, rounding is to the nearest $120 (so that the monthly test will be in rounded $10 units).

Finally, let us look at the actual past history as to the operations of the automatics in connection with the maximum taxable earnings base and the earnings test. The 1974 earnings base of $13,200 was multiplied by the increase of 5.9445 percent in the average taxable wage per employee with wages for the first quarter of 1974 over the corresponding average for the first quarter of 1973 (i.e., $2,007.69 as compared with $1,895.04);[21] the result was $13,984.67, and this

---

[19] The test described is applicable in the United States, or abroad if in covered employment. A different test is applicable for other employment abroad (based on days of work in the month for which benefits are payable).

[20] This term is not defined in the law, but rather by regulations. It does not involve the amount of self-employment earnings, but rather the time spent in self-employment, which limit varies depending upon the skills of the person. Before the 1977 Amendments, the monthly test applied to all years of benefit receipt.

[21] In order to meet the initial legal requirement of making the promulgation by November 1 of the year before the new base would be effective, these first-quarter average wages are

was then rounded to $14,100, which was the 1975 earnings base. The latter was then multiplied by the increase of 7.4733 percent for the average first-quarter taxable wage from 1974 to 1975 (when such average was $2,157.73); the result was $15,153.74, which was rounded to $15,300 as the 1976 earnings base. As indicated previously, the same factor was used for determining the 1977 earnings base, which is thus $16,500 ($15,300 increased by 7.4733 percent is $16,443.41). For 1978, the determination was based on an increase of 6.9003 percent (based on a first-quarter 1976 average wage of $2,306.62), yielding $17,638.55, which was rounded to $17,700.

In the same manner, the monthly exempt amount in the earnings test for 1975 was obtained by increasing the $200 amount for 1974 by 5.9445 percent, to yield $211.89, which was rounded to $210 (with the corresponding annual exempt amount being $2,520). Then, the monthly exempt amount for 1976 was $210 increased by 7.4733 percent, to yield $225.69, which was rounded to $230 (with the annual exempt amount being $2,760). For 1977, the monthly exempt amount was determined using the same factor as for 1976, with a result of $247.19, which was rounded to $250 (with the annual exempt amount being $3,000).

Similarly, for 1978, the increase of 6.9003 percent was applied to $250 to yield $267.75, which was rounded to $270, with the annual exempt amount being $3,240. The 1977 Amendments provided, however, that for beneficiaries aged 65 and over (effective for the entire year when age 65 is attained), ad hoc increases in the exempt amounts would be made. On an annual basis, these are $4,000 for 1978, with $500 increases each year until, in 1982, $6,000 is to be applicable, with automatic adjustments thereafter.

METHOD OF INCREASING REQUIREMENT FOR QUARTERS OF COVERAGE

Eligibility for benefits is based on obtaining an insured status, and this in turn is based on the number of "quarters of coverage"

computed on the basis of the total taxable wages and the number of employees involved as determined from the data for the first quarter which had been reported and posted to the Summary Earnings Records by the end of the quarterly updating completed in September. Because of the change in the law introducing a longer lag (as is necessary when annual data from the annual-reporting procedure, effective for 1978, are to be used), such tight deadline was not present for the determinations for 1976 and after. For 1973, 70.6 million employees were so included; while for 1974, 1975, and 1976, the corresponding numbers were 71.1, 70.6, and 72.8 million, respectively.

which the individual has acquired, as against the requirements of the law. Ever since 1940 and until the 1977 Amendments, the general requirement for a quarter of coverage was having $50 or more of wages in covered employment be paid in a calendar quarter. The fact that the $50 amount was not changed for more than 35 years, despite wage levels being about nine times higher, meant that it became increasingly easier to obtain credit for a quarter of coverage (i.e., there was a hidden liberalization of the program).

The 1977 Amendments changed the basis of determining quarters of coverage. This was done, at least in part, because beginning in 1968, earnings will be reported on an annual basis, rather than quarterly, for the vast majority of workers (all except domestic employees and state and local government employees). For 1978, one quarter of coverage is credited for each full $250 of credited earnings. Thus, $1,000 or more of earnings in a year will produce four quarters of coverage for that year.

The $250 figure is to be adjusted for future years in exactly the same manner as the maximum taxable earnings base and the exempt amount in the earnings test—by changes in the average annual wage of all workers in the country. The result is rounded to the nearest $10, and no decrease is permitted from the previous year's figure if the average wage decreases. For example, for 1979, if the average nationwide wage increases by 7 percent from 1976 to 1977, the requirement for a quarter of coverage would be $270 (rounded up from the resulting computed $267.50). If the average wage had decreased from 1976 to 1977, the requirement would have remained at $250 (and the measurement of the change for the 1980 requirement would have been as between the average wages in 1976 and 1978).

METHOD OF INCREASING MAXIMUM APPLICABLE TO DISABILITY BENEFITS WHEN WORKERS' COMPENSATION BENEFITS ALSO PAYABLE

Another instance where social security benefits are automatically adjusted for changes in economic conditions occurs in connection with disability beneficiaries who are also receiving workers' compensation benefits for work-connected injury or disease

(WC). An offset may be made against the social security benefit, which is done so that total benefit income would not be so large as to possibly discourage rehabilitation and return to work.[22] Such offset is only applicable before age 62 (and not to survivor benefits in any case), and not then if the WC program itself has provision for an offset of social security benefits. As will be described hereafter, such offset provision has an automatic-adjustment feature, which was adopted in 1965 and thus was the forerunner of the automatic-adjustment provisions described previously and, in fact, served as a precedent therefor.

The offset applies whenever the total of the two benefits (including any social security dependents benefits) exceeds 80 percent of "Average Current Earnings" (ACE).[23] After the beneficiary has been on the roll for two full calendar years after the year when the offset was first applied, the "80 percent of ACE" maximum is subject to increase to reflect the change in the general earnings level. The same procedure is followed every three years thereafter. The theory underlying this is that any disincentive to return to work is related to the general earnings level prevailing at the time of benefit receipt. Rather anomalously and inconsistently, the social security benefit considered is that initially payable, and not the increased benefit due to ad hoc or automatic increases made subsequently that is actually payable.

The ACE is automatically adjusted in exactly the same manner as is the maximum taxable earnings base and the exempt amounts in the earnings test, except that no benefit-increase trigger is required and that adjustment is not made annually but rather only triennially. Before the change to annual reporting of wages was made in legislation in early 1976 (effective first for 1978), whenever the ACE was to be increased for a year, this was done from first-

---

[22] During the legislative development of the 1977 Amendments, the Senate deleted this offset, but the conference committee between the House and the Senate restored it, and the final legislation therefore retained it.

[23] Average Current Earnings is the largest of (a) the Average Monthly Wage or, under the 1977 Amendments, for those disabled after 1978, the Average Indexed Monthly Earnings (as used to compute social security benefits generally); (b) the monthly average of total earnings in covered employment in the highest five consecutive years of earnings after 1950; and (c) the highest such monthly average for any year in the last six years before disablement. Item (c) will usually be applicable, although when the AIME is used in item (a), it may instead be applicable.

quarter taxable-wage data.[24] For example, if a disabled worker first received disability benefits in 1966 and was subject to the offset and had an ACE of $200, then for 1969 the worker's ACE was increased, which resulted in increased benefits because there was then a smaller offset. The 1969 ACE was determined by multiplying the original $200 ACE by the increase of 13.8 percent in the average wage per wage item for the first quarter of 1968 over that for 1966 ($1,219 and $1,071, respectively), which yields $227.[25] Similarily, the ACE was redetermined for 1972—on the basis of the increase in the average wage item for the first quarter of 1971 over that for 1968.[26]

METHOD OF INCREASING MEDICARE PREMIUM RATES

Closely related to the matter of increasing social security benefits is an automatic-adjustment provision relating to the determination of the annual standard premium rate under the Supplementary Medical Insurance (SMI) portion of the Medicare program, often referred to as Part B.[27] SMI provides for the payment or reimbursement of part of the medical-care costs for physicians and certain related services for individuals who are aged 65 or over or who have been receiving social security benefits on the basis of

---

[24] Actually, the precise methodology used for the adjustment of the earnings base and the earnings test (beginning with 1975, using 1973 and 1974 data) was not initially followed for the WC offset. Instead, data more readily available were used to approximate this element, since only a small group of persons was involved. Specifically, what was used was the average wage per first-quarter wage item, which is the quarterly report that each employer makes for each employee. Thus, some employees have more than one wage item in a quarter. The trend of this average was probably little different than that of the average wage per employee, which naturally was at a somewhat higher level.

[25] Just as in the case of the Average Monthly Wage (as used to compute social security benefits generally), the adjusted ACE, if not an even dollar, is always rounded down to the next lower dollar.

[26] The data for the average wage per wage item for the first quarters of various years back through 1965, when this procedure first became effective, may be found in Robert J. Myers, *Social Security* (Homewood, Ill.: Richard D. Irwin, Inc., 1975), p. 124.

[27] In general, the enrollee must pay the first $60 of annual costs recognized by the program and 20 percent of the remainder, with SMI paying the remainder of the cost; it is important to note, however, that SMI does not necessarily recognize all of the charges for medical services, so that the enrollee must also pay the excess of the actual charges over the recognized ones, unless the provider of services has accepted an assignment (and so is paid SMI's payment directly by the program). For more details of the SMI benefit provisions, see Robert J. Myers, *Social Security* (Homewood, Ill.: Richard D. Irwin, Inc., 1975), pp. 221–56.

disability for at least two years and who elect to participate and pay premiums.[28] It began operation in July 1966.

One reason for the shift from Januarys to Junes for the effective date of social security benefit increases under the automatics was to have coordination with increases in the SMI standard enrolled premium rate. Such premiums are predominantly collected each month in advance by deduction from the monthly social security benefit payable at the beginning of the month (with respect to the previous month); persons not on the benefit roll, who are almost always engaged in substantial employment, pay quarterly. The premium rate for the 12-month period beginning each July is determined in the preceding December. Accordingly, any increase in the premium rate will first show up in the social security check for June, which is paid to the beneficiary at the beginning of July.

Indexing of social security benefits also has an effect on the SMI premium rate. Such rate is based, in principle, on 50 percent of the estimated cost of the SMI benefits and associated administrative expenses for persons aged 65 and over. However, beginning with the premium rate for the period July 1973 through June 1974, there has been the limitation that the percentage increase in the rate from one year to the next cannot exceed the increase in the general level of social security benefits.[29] This limitation is measured, in the December preceding the premium period, on the basis of the increase in social security benefits from the preceding May to what will be payable for the coming May (as the law stands in such December).

Thus, if an automatic benefit increase occurs in the preceding June, the percentage thereof will be applicable as a maximum possible increase in the SMI premium rate. For example, the monthly premium rate for the period beginning July 1976 would have been $10.70 for persons aged 65 and over on the "normal" 50 percent basis, but instead the increase was held to $7.20 on the basis of the

---

[28] The standard premium rate is that charged to eligible persons who enroll on a timely basis. Late enrollees pay a surcharge of 10 percent for each full year of delay in enrolling.

[29] Such increase is measured for promulgations before that to be made in December 1979 for a person with a benefit based on an AMW of $750, while for that promulgation and subsequent ones it is measured for a person with an AIME of $900. This specific designation has no real effect if the benefit increase arises under the automatics—since the same percentage applies to all benefits—but rather only if there is an ad hoc change with varying increases at different benefit levels.

8.0 percent social security benefit increase applied to the previous $6.70 (and rounded to the nearest dime). It is likely that this limitation will be applicable for some years to come. The deficiency between the 50 percent share of the SMI premium and what the enrollee actually pays—as well as the 50 percent share—is met from general revenues of the federal government.

As a result, it is very likely that any increase in the SMI premium rate will be more than offset by the automatic increase in the social security benefits.[30] For example, the SMI premium rate increased from $6.70 to $7.20 for July 1976. This 50-cent increase was overshadowed by the 6.4 percent benefit increase coming due in the same check, which was $6.50 for a person receiving the minimum primary benefit.

Not only does this coordination of the automatic benefit increase with the increases in the SMI premium rate simplify administration by having only one change in the amount of the check in a year instead of two, but also it results in less dissatisfaction and lack of understanding on the part of the beneficiaries.

Under certain circumstances, persons not insured under the Hospital Insurance portion of Medicare can obtain such protection by voluntary election of coverage and payment of premiums. Such premium rate, too, is automatically adjusted annually. The method for doing so is described in the next section.

METHOD OF INCREASING MEDICARE COST-SHARING PROVISIONS

The Hospital Insurance (HI) portion of the Medicare program contains certain cost-sharing provisions relating to the benefit protection, which are automatically adjusted each year.[31] Such automatic adjustment is, in essence, negative benefit indexing.

HI covers all services furnished by hospitals and certain other institutions after hospitalization has ended. Certain cost-sharing payments are required from the covered persons (who must be

---

[30] Under certain circumstances, there could be an increase in the SMI premium rate, but no rise in the level of social security benefits. This would result for a period beginning with a particular July if there had been an automatic increase in benefits for the second preceding June, but thereafter the CPI had stabilized considerably (or not increased very much) and the costs of the SMI program had risen somewhat (or else the previous premium rate had not been at the full 50 percent basis).

[31] For more details of the eligibility conditions and benefit provisions of the HI system, see the source cited in footnote 27.

aged 65 or over or have been receiving social security benefits on the basis of disability for at least two years). It began operation in July 1966.

Specifically, initially for 1966–68, the basic cost-sharing amount was established by law at $40 (which, by coincidence, was approximately the average daily cost of all hospital services, averaged out both over all durations of hospitalization and over all hospitals in the country). Such basic amount is utilized in several ways.

An initial deductible upon entering a hospital (and thus establishing a so-called "spell of illness") equal to the basic amount is imposed—and also for each subsequent spell of illness.[32] After the first 60 days of hospitalization in a spell of illness, the individual must pay a cost-sharing amount equal to 25 percent of the basic amount for each of the next 30 days. Beyond 90 days of hospitalization in a spell of illness, benefits are payable only from a 60-day lifetime reserve (which is independent of spells of illness). Such days, voluntarily used, require daily cost sharing of 50 percent of the basic amount. Care provided in a skilled nursing facility after hospitalization is subject to cost sharing of 12½ percent of the basic amount for each of the next 80 days after the first such 20 days in a spell of illness (no benefits provided after the 100th day).

After 1968, the basic cost-sharing amount as it relates to a spell of illness beginning in a subsequent year is adjusted automatically, with the promulgation being made between July 1 and October 1 of the preceding year. The procedure applicable to a particular year is to multiply the initial amount of $40 by the ratio of (a) the average daily cost for covered inpatient hospital services with respect to insured persons[33] for the second preceding year to (b) such average daily cost for 1966. The result is then rounded to the nearest multiple of $4 (so that the daily cost-sharing amounts applicable to hospital benefits are in even dollars). For example, the basic cost-

---

[32] A "spell of illness" is defined as the period beginning with the first day of hospitalization and ending after the individual has been out of both hospitals and skilled nursing facilities for 60 consecutive days.

[33] The term "insured persons" relates only to those who are eligible for HI benefits as a result of their insured status for social security benefits (including not only insured workers but also eligible dependents and survivors). It thus does not include persons blanketed-in for HI benefits who were not so insured (principally persons who attained age 65 before 1968 and who were not eligible for health benefits as federal employees and who were not short-term nonresident aliens, plus a few persons who attained age 65 after 1967 and had some specified amounts of covered employment but not enough to be insured) or persons who voluntarily enrolled in HI on a premium-paying basis.

sharing amount of $104 applicable for spells of illness beginning in 1976 was derived from $40 times $97.93 (the 1974 average daily cost), divided by $37.92 (the 1966 average daily cost), which yields $103.32.

As mentioned previously, the HI program permits individuals who are not insured (or who, despite not being insured, were blanketed-in at its inception) to elect coverage by paying a premium therefor. The standard premium rate was established by law at $33 for the initial year of operation, July 1973 through June 1974.[34] Thereafter, such rate is automatically determined in October–December of a particular year for the 12-month period beginning with the next July. The same general basis is used as for the basic cost-sharing amount. Specifically, the monthly rate for the 12-month period beginning with July of a particular year is obtained by multiplying $33 by the ratio of (*a*) the basic cost-sharing amount determined for the particular year to (*b*) such amount for 1973,[35] with the result being rounded to the nearest even dollar. For example, the rate of $45 for the year beginning July 1976 was derived from $33, times $104, divided by $76, which equals $45.16 (which was rounded to $45).

It can thus be seen that, in essence, the HI voluntary-coverage premium rate is automatically adjusted according to changes in the level of covered hospital services. The extent to which the small group involved pays its own way,[36] which was the congressional intent, depends upon other factors than the trend in hospital costs—for example, on whether the initial premium rate was adequate and on its relative utilization of services. For the first two years of operation, the per capita cost for benefits and administrative expenses was approximately equal to the premium rates, but after then it appears that the per capita cost will exceed the premium rates.[37]

---

[34] The standard premium rate is that charged to eligible persons who enroll on a timely basis. Late enrollees pay a surcharge of 10 percent for each full year of delay in enrolling.

[35] Actually in practice, the HI basic cost-sharing amount in 1973 was $72, although it was computed, according to the provisions of the law, at $76. Such action was to comply with a ruling of the Cost of Living Council (which, in my opinion, was illogical, and possibly illegal as well). Quite properly, the amount for 1973 computed according to the provisions of the law has been used as the base point for future computations of the voluntary-coverage premium rate.

[36] In 1976, only 17,000 persons were in this category.

[37] See "1976 HI Trustees Report," *House Document No. 94-502,* May 24, 1976, p. 32.

If the HI voluntary-coverage premium rate is desired to be at a self-supporting level, then it may well be necessary for legislative action to be taken to increase it further than the automatic-adjustment provisions would do. This could be accomplished either by a one-time ad hoc increase (with the present automatic-adjustment provisions applying thereafter) or by changing the basis to an annual promulgation one, as in the case of the SMI premium rate.[38] On the other hand, from a public-policy standpoint, and also to prevent the possible upward snowballing of the premium rate if antiselection were to occur as the premium rate was increased much more rapidly than hospital costs, the deficiencies resulting from an inadequate rate could, without any significant or noticeable effect, be easily borne by the HI Trust Fund from its very much larger other sources of income (payroll taxes and interest receipts).

In passing, it should be noted that the SMI initial deductible of $60 per year is not automatically adjusted to reflect changing economic conditions. Initially, it was $50 (beginning for July–December 1966) and was changed on an ad hoc basis to $60 by legislation in 1972 (effective for 1973). In hindsight at least, this deductible should have been subject to indexing, just as were the HI cost-sharing provisions.

President Ford, in both 1975 and 1976, recommended that the SMI initial deductible should be automatically adjusted in proportion with changes in the general level of social security cash benefits. The effect would be to increase the deductible as medical costs rise, although not necessarily at exactly the same rate. Congress did not act on these proposals.

POSSIBLE CHANGES IN AUTOMATIC-ADJUSTMENT PROVISIONS

Let us now look at the possible changes that have been discussed or proposed in connection with the automatic adjustment of various portions of the social security program, other than those as to indexing and decoupling the benefit computation procedure for new awards (as dealt with in the previous section). Nor will there be any discussion of possible changes in the automatic-adjustment

---

[38] Such an annual-promulgation procedure, based on projected likely future experience, would have been very difficult to have followed in the early years of operation because of unavailability of data for the very small group involved.

provisions applicable to the Medicare program because these have been mentioned previously.

It is generally agreed that the automatics have worked out quite satisfactorily as to the maximum taxable earnings base and the exempt amounts in the earnings test. Some persons advocate that such elements should currently be at a much higher level, but they do not advocate any change in the method of adjusting them after any such increase is made.

Several changes have, however, been suggested as to the automatic adjustment of benefit amounts for those on the roll. When double-digit inflation was present in 1974–75, it was proposed that adjustment should be made more frequently than annually. One possibility is to do this on a semiannual basis (as was done in the Senate version of the 1977 Amendments, but was deleted from the legislation as enacted; under this proposal, the adjustment would be made after six months *only* if the CPI increases at least 4 percent, as against the 3 percent required for the annual increases). Another possibility is to use the "trigger" procedure—that is, adjustment would take place, after such administrative lag as necessary, as soon as the CPI rises by a certain amount (such as 3 percent) from the previous base point.

Now that inflation is at a lower level, pressure for such changes has diminished, and there would seem no reason to change from the annual basis as long as inflation is at an annual rate of, say, 6 percent or less. More frequent adjustment, and especially when not on a routinized basis (such as always for June) can result in great administrative problems for a program having millions of beneficiaries.

Question has been raised from time to time about the appropriateness of the CPI for keeping social security benefits up to date with changing economic conditions. There is, of course, always such a problem in connection with any average. Living costs and their distribution among various types of expenditures differ greatly as between different persons, depending upon such elements as home ownership, health, geographical location, and income level.

The vast majority of the social security beneficiaries are aged 60 or over, and their expenditures patterns are quite different from those of the urban families for whom the new CPI is determined. Older persons, for example, tend to have higher medical costs;

however, for those aged 65 or over, Medicare offsets much of this difference. No valid substitute for the CPI to apply to social security beneficiaries has been developed as yet, although there has been some attempt to do so. Moreover, what is important is not the level of any such index but rather its relative changes over time. From this latter standpoint, it seems that the general CPI is an adequate tool. The 1977 Amendments provide, however, that this subject is to be studied further by the National Commission on Social Security (created by such legislation).

The view has been expressed, however, that the concept of keeping social security benefits up to date with prices is not sufficient. Such procedure has the purpose of maintaining their "real" purchasing power. Some believe that more than this should be done for the beneficiaries—namely, that their benefits should reflect the current increases in productivity as well. This could be accomplished by indexing by changes in wage levels (as is done for the earnings base and the exempt amounts in the earnings test and as is the case for the earnings records and the bands in the benefit formula under the wage-indexing decoupling approach), rather than by changes in the CPI.

Technically, this indexing of benefits in force by changes in the wage level could readily be done. It does, however, raise questions as to the underlying philosophy of the benefit structure and its purposes. Also involved are cost considerations because this approach would likely have significantly higher costs. For example, if the differential between increases in wages and increases in prices were 2 percent each year, the overall cost of the program would be about 10 percent higher relatively. Of course, if over any considerable period of years, wages increased less rapidly than prices, the reverse situation would prevail, and wage indexing would be disadvantageous to the beneficiaries; under such circumstances, there would be a serious question as to whether the present CPI indexing for benefits in current payment is appropriate (and is equitable to covered workers who are paying the costs involved).

Indexing of Benefits of Federal Employee Retirement Systems and Other Federal Benefits and of Workers' Compensation Benefits

A wide variety of governmental benefit programs in the United States contain provisions for adjusting benefits to reflect changes in the cost of living. Diverse procedures are followed, in part because of different goals or needs of the particular program and in part by "happenstance." The experience in this respect under the social security (OASDI) and railroad retirement programs has been described and analyzed in the previous chapter. This chapter will deal with all other federal governmental programs, and with the state workers' compensation systems.

FEDERAL STAFF RETIREMENT SYSTEMS

Adjustments on an Ad Hoc Basis

Before 1962, retirement pensions for federal civilian employees were not generally subject to increases to reflect changes in the cost of living, or, conversely, the decreasing real value of the pension as prices rose. Occasionally, ad hoc adjustments were made to reflect the fact that the salary levels in the past had been so much lower than current ones, which determine the pensions of those currently retiring. In somewhat the same vein, at times the program was liberalized (as for example, when the benefit rate per year of service was increased), but this did not apply to persons already on the pension roll.

The theory underlying this approach, which often created considerable inequities as between border cases (persons retiring just before or just after the effective date), was an analogy to private insurance on an individual basis. Thus, it was asserted—incorrectly, in the author's opinion, from a broad pension-design viewpoint—that individuals who had already retired before the change had "bought and paid for" their benefit provisions and so were not "entitled" to any liberalization thereof. Quite naturally, such actions created considerable dissatisfaction on the part of those affected adversely, and palliative partial changes were sometimes subsequently adopted.[1]

One exception to the foregoing situation of nonadjustment of the pensions of civilian employees once they had gone on the roll was in the case of certain special groups such as federal judges, for whom the pension was a stipulated proportion of the *current* salary of the position previously held. In such cases, of course, any changes in economic or other conditions that resulted in an increase in salaries for active members carried through to the retired members. In a similar manner, under legislation enacted in 1958 (3 U.S.C. 102), former presidents receive a pension equal in amount to the basic pay of the head of an executive department (i.e., a secretary) at whatever rate that is current—$66,000 at the end of 1977.

From the very beginning of the military retirement system,[2] the benefit amounts were related to the current salary of the particular grade at which the individual retired. As a result, there was automatic adjustment of military pensions, which are termed "retired

---

[1] For example, Public Law 369 of 1955 increased the annuities under the Civil Service Retirement Act for those who retired before 1958; this was done so as to reflect the approximately 8 percent salary increases, which were in part to recognize cost-of-living changes. The increases for those who retired before July 1955 were 12 percent of the first $1,500 of annual annuity, plus 8 percent of the excess, subject to the increased annuity not exceeding $4,104 (those retiring in July 1955 to December 1957 received phased-in smaller increases). As another example, Public Law 85-465 of 1958 increased the CSR annuities of those who retired before October 1956 by 10 percent (subject to a maximum increase of $500 a year), so as to recognize, in part, that subsequent retirees had a much more liberal benefit formula applicable.

[2] The term "military retirement system" as used here includes not only the program applicable to the armed forces but also the programs for commissioned officers in the Public Health Service and for the National Oceanic and Atmospheric Administration (formerly, the Coast Guard), which have the same provisions as the former.

pay." How well this automatic adjustment kept pace with the cost of living depended upon the trend of military salaries as compared with that of prices. Military retired pay has always been determined on a final-salary basis, from the last month's pay rate. It should be especially noted that benefits payable with respect to veterans of military service by the Veterans Administration are not part of the military retirement system; such benefits have always been adjusted on an ad hoc basis by Congress, but in mid-1978, legislation was pending that would adjust these benefits in exactly the same manner as OASDI benefits are adjusted (H.R. 10173).

Thus, until 1958 the retired pay of those on the roll was automatically adjusted according to changes in the active-duty pay scale. For example, the retired pay of a retiree who had left service as a colonel was always the same for a particular month as that for a colonel with the same length of service who retired in that month. In other words, the salary used in computing the pension for a retiree was always the same as that payable to active-duty personnel in the same grade with the same length of service.

From 1958 to 1963, military retired pay for those on the roll was "uncoupled" from the active-duty pay structure and certain arbitrary percentage increases were given (such increases being lower than the pay increases). Then, in 1963, provisions were enacted for automatic increases based on changes in the Consumer Price Index (Public Law 88-132). Since then, there have been automatic-adjustment provisions following the precedent of the Civil Service Retirement system (as will be described subsequently).

The type of "coupling" between active-duty pay and the salary used currently for computing retired pay under the military retirement system that was used before 1958 had the advantage of consistency and smooth-junction treatment as between current retirees, recent retirees, and those who have been on the roll for a long time. As contrasted with adjusting retired pay on the basis of changes in the cost of living (as measured, say, by the CPI), the current-pay adjustment method is *generally* more favorable to the retirees because in most of the economic history of the United States, salaries have increased much more rapidly than prices.

But such was not the case for military personnel during the time when their retired pay was adjusted on the basis of the current active-duty pay scale. In the period 1908–58, for example, their salaries increased by 224 percent, but the general level of wages in the country, as measured by average hourly wages for production workers in manufacturing, increased by 1,040 percent. The CPI rose by 225 percent in the period. In fact, during almost all years in this 50-year period, the index for military pay was about the same or lower than the index for the CPI, the base for both being 100 in 1908.

In the period after 1958 (when military retired pay was adjusted more or less on the basis of price changes rather than active-duty pay changes), as it so happens, active-duty pay rose much more rapidly than the CPI, until about 1972. Since then, the reverse has occurred. As a result, retirees under the pay scales in effect from April 1955 through 1971 were not as well off as they would have been under the previous adjustment basis (coupled to the active-duty pay structure). The reverse, to a small extent, was the case for retirees in 1972–74, since the CPI then increased more rapidly than did active-duty pay.

The foregoing discussion is intended to be only a presentation of the factual situation. It should not be construed as arguing for or against automatic-adjustment procedures under the military retirement system. Certainly, these procedures can, on the whole, be said to be proper, equitable, and logical.

Specifically as to the actual situation for military retirees in 1958–74, on the average those who retired in 1955 were about 31 percent *worse off* in 1975 under the actual situation as to automatic-adjustment procedures than if the adjustments had been made on the basis of active-duty pay. This "disadvantage" decreases for subsequent retirements until, for those who retired at the beginning of 1972, it disappeared, that is, such individuals were about as well off under either adjustment basis. Subsequent retirements up to October 1974, when a new pay scale was instituted, were actually about 3 percent *better off* under the adjustment procedure in present law, as against how they would have fared under the active-duty pay adjustment method.

The foregoing situation led to demands that there should be a recomputation procedure instituted for individuals who retired before 1972, such that their retired pay *in the future* would, under certain circumstances, be recomputed on the basis of the salary scale first instituted on January 1, 1972. Such retired pay as so recomputed would include CPI increases just as though retirement had occurred on January 1, 1972, but would never result in a decrease in the amount as computed under present law. The recomputation would be effective generally only for retirees aged 60 and over and for retirees with at least a 30 percent disability, regardless of age. For those now under age 60 and not so disabled, the recomputation would be made in the future when age 60 is attained. Such a proposal was contained, for example, in the Senate version of the Defense Appropriation Act for Fiscal Year 1975 (as Title VII thereof), but it was dropped out in the joint conference between the House of Representatives and the Senate. It was also contained in H.R. 12505 (February 4, 1974), a bill entitled "Uniformed Services Retirement Modernization Act." Since then, no legislative action along these lines has occurred.

Automatic Adjustments Prior to 1976[3]

In the early 1960s, a movement began to introduce automatic-adjustment provisions for pensions in force under the Civil Service Retirement system (CSR). It should be noted that under this program there is no significant problem about the initial amount generally being up to date relative to recent earnings because it is based, in essence, on final wages.[4] Considering that the cost of living, as measured by the Consumer Price Index, was relatively stable in the early 1960s, it is surprising that there was this pressure for indexing of pensions. In fact, it is interesting and significant that the extensive review of all federal retirement systems conducted by authorization of Congress in 1954 by the Committee on Retirement Policy for Federal Personnel (the so-called Kaplan Committee) did not even mention the subject of automatic-adjustment provisions.[5]

In a subsequent review of federal retirement systems made in 1966 by an intragovernment group, the Cabinet Committee on Federal Staff Retirement Systems, the conclusion was reached that the automatic-adjustment system then in effect for CSR and the military retirement system was quite satisfactory and adequately maintained the purchasing power of the benefits. Accordingly, the Cabinet Committee recommended that this procedure be extended

[3] For an excellent account of the legislative history of these provisions (as well as similar ones in other plans for governmental employees), see John P. Mackin, "Protecting Purchasing Power in Retirement," (New York: Fleet Academic Editions, Inc., 1971).

[4] In the early 1960s, the average salary for pension computation purposes was based on the highest five consecutive years of service. Currently, a three-year average is used.

[5] "Retirement Policy for Federal Personnel," *Senate Document No. 89*, 1954.

to the various smaller federal retirement systems. The Cabinet Committee also took the position that federal retirement benefits should not be increased in relation to changes in salary levels (as had formerly been done in the military retirement system), as some had proposed and that any further liberalization of the procedure was unwarranted.[6]

Public Law 87-793 (1962) provided that CSR annuities in force at the beginning of 1963 would be increased 5 percent, with progressively smaller increases for new retirees coming on the roll in each of the next four years. Automatic cost-of-living increases based on the CPI were initiated. Establishment of this relationship between living costs and benefits was intended to provide a permanent solution to a recurring problem. Increases in benefits would be related directly to increases in the CPI.

Individuals who are separated from service before attaining the minimum retirement age (currently, age 55 with 30 years of service, age 60 with 20 years of service, and age 62 with 5 years of service) can elect to receive a vested deferred annuity at age 62 if they have at least 5 years of service and do not request a refund of their contributions. The amount of the pension is currently based on the high three-year average salary and the years of service and is subject to automatic cost-of-living increases *only* after age 62, when the pension is payable.

The basis for the automatic increase was the calendar-year average of the monthly CPI, with benefits increased whenever the cumulative rise was at least 3 percent. Increases, rounded to the nearest $1/10$ percent, would be effective in April of the year following the increase. The first base year was 1962, and each subsequent increase would introduce a new base year.

Under these provisions (and under all provisions discussed in this section), the automatic adjustment operates only in an upward direction. In other words, when the CPI decreases, benefits are not adjusted downward. Of course, under such circumstances, any subsequent increase in benefits is not measured from the lowest CPI following the prior base point, but rather from such base point.

A similar approach was shortly thereafter applied in the military retirement system, which had switched to the cost-of-living proce-

---

[6] "Federal Staff Retirement Systems—Report to the President of the United States by the Cabinet Committee on Federal Staff Retirement Systems," *House Document No. 402,* 89th Cong., March 7, 1966, p. 13.

dure on an ad hoc basis in 1958, after more than a century of using the "corresponding salary level" procedure. Public Law 88-132 (1963) included a 5 percent increase in military retirement benefits (based on the 1958–62 increase in the CPI), permitted recomputation of benefits for retirements before the June 1958 pay increase in lieu of the percentage increase, and provided automatic cost-of-living increases in military retirement benefits thereafter, on the same basis as those provided for CSR. It was then made clear by Congress that there would be no further recomputation of military benefits on the basis of increased active-duty pay increases, but instead cost-of-living adjustments would be made.

Legislation in 1965 provided for modifications in the automatic cost-of-living adjustments for both military retirement (Public Law 89-132, August 21, 1965) and CSR (Public Law 89-205, September 27, 1965) in order to reduce the time lag between increases in the CPI and their reflection in the monthly benefits. No increase in benefits had occurred in 1964–65 (the increase over the 1962 CPI was only 2.6 percent in 1964). The prospective 1965 increase of about 4 percent would not have been applied to benefits until April 1966.

The 1965 legislation provided benefit increases under both programs to compensate for this time lag. Also, the cost-of-living adjustment was revised. Whenever the CPI would rise at least 3 percent for three consecutive months above that for the month used as a base for the last previous cost-of-living increase, benefits commencing before the effective date would be increased. Such increase is effective for the third month following the three-month period. The amount of the increase is the percentage rise in the CPI in the highest of the three months over the CPI for the prior base month. The first base month was July 1965 for CSR benefits and September 1965 for military retirement benefits.

A specific example may make it clearer how this automatic-adjustment provision had operated. Suppose that the last previous base period was February 1968 and that the CPI first increased by at least 3.0 percent thereafter in April 1969 and at least this increase prevailed during the next two months. Then, the month in April–June 1969 with the highest CPI was the new base period, and the increase based thereon was first payable with respect to September 1969.

Public Law 89-488 (1966) added the same provision to the Federal Employees Compensation (FEC) program, which provides workers' compensation benefits for work-connected injuries and disease. Such provision was effective for awards based on injury or death at least a year before the effective date of the increase, so that the three programs had adjustment provisions that were identical except for the first base month and for the initial deferment for a year under FEC.

In the years following 1963, several of the smaller retirement systems for federal employees adopted the same automatic-adjustment provisions as those applicable to CSR.[7] Such systems were the Foreign Service Retirement System and those of the Central Intelligence Agency, District of Columbia teachers, District of Columbia judges, Former Lighthouse Service, Board of Governors of the Federal Reserve System (a nonstatutory plan for this group of quasi-federal employees of such Board of Governors, which plan exactly parallels CSR, but with the automatic-adjustment provision not being on a contractual basis),[8] and the survivor pensions for District of Columbia fire fighters and police (including the Executive Protective Service and the Park Police).[9]

The adjustment procedure in the military retirement system was refined by Public Law 90-207 (1967) to assure that persons with the same basic pay and length of service receive the same retired pay and that persons who retire after a pay increase or after a cost-of-living increase receive benefits adjusted to reflect the effect of those increases.

If there is a general pay increase after a base month, the next increase for retired pay that is based on the increased pay rates is limited to the increase in the CPI for the current base month over the CPI for the month preceding the pay increase (instead of that for the prior base month). For example, if the last previous base

---

[7] See "Automatic Cost-of-Living Increases in Federal Programs," Office of Management and Budget, Executive Office of the President, *Technical Paper Series BRD/FAB 75-2*, July 30, 1975.

[8] There is a separate plan for employees of the several Federal Reserve banks throughout the country which can properly be considered as a private pension plan. It provides ad hoc, noncontractual adjustments of pensions in course of payment, which in the past have closely approximated the changes in the CPI. The same situation occurs for the quasi-federal employees of the several military post-exchange systems.

[9] The retirement benefits for District of Columbia fire fighters and police are, like the previous practice of the military retirement system, based on the current pay of the rank held by the retiree.

month were March 1969, and if there were a general pay increase in September 1969, then let us consider persons retiring after August 1969. If a new base month were established for May 1970, the CPI increase would be measured from August 1969 to May 1970 (not from March 1969 to May 1970, as would be done for those who retired before September 1969).

Under the circumstances that no general pay increase occurs after a particular base month and before retirement, then for retirement occurring after the base month, the benefit is increased by the ratio of the CPI for such base month to the CPI for the month preceding the last pay increase (except as to any months prior to the effective date based on such base month; for those months, the preceding base month is applicable in determining the increase). For example, if the last previous base month were March 1969, and if there were a general pay increase in January 1969, then let us

TABLE 4
Determination of Cost-of-Living Increases in Federal Benefits Based on Increases in the Consumer Price Index as They Were before 1 Percent Add-On Was Eliminated in 1976

Item	Military Retirement	Civil Service Retirement*	Federal Employees Compensation	Social Security
Base is period of	1 month	1 month	1 month	First quarter of calendar year
New base requires 3 percent rise in CPI (over prior base†) in	3 consecutive months	3 consecutive months	3 consecutive months	First quarter average
Current base is	High month	High month	High month	Quarterly average
Increase in benefits:				
Equal to percent rise in CPI, current base over prior base§	Plus 1%‡	Plus 1%	As so computed	As so computed
Effective first of	Third month after 3-month period	Third month after 3-month period	Third month after 3-month period	Following June
Applies for	Retirement before effective date‖	Retirement before effective date	Injury 1 year before effective date	All retirements (past and future)

* Also applies to Foreign Service Retirement system and several other small systems (see text).

† Prior base is period for which the CPI was the basis of the last previous cost-of-living increase.

‡ If retired on pay which was increased after prior base, the month preceding the pay increase is substituted for the prior base.

§ Rounded to the nearest 1/10 percent.

‖ There is also an immediate increase in benefits upon retirement *after* the effective date that is equal to the percentage increase in CPI for the base that determined the cost-of-living increase over that for the month preceding the most recent pay increase.

consider persons retiring after June 1969. The benefit increase initially for this category is determined from the ratio of the CPI for March 1969 to that for December 1968. Thus, the initial benefit reflects rises in the CPI between the last pay increase and the most recent cost-of-living adjustment in benefits before retirement. The results of this complex, but logical and equitable, procedure can perhaps be more easily understood by studying Tables 4 and 5.

Thus, under the military retirement system, quite logically, a smaller increase in retired pay results if retirement occurs after a general pay increase and before a cost-of-living increase than if there had been no general pay increase after the cost-of-living in-

TABLE 5
Description of Initial Adjustments under Military Retirement System for Various Circumstances

A. *First Month of Retirement Immediately Preceded by (or Concurrent with) Base Month*
   1. Payments for months before third month after base month (if any such months)—increase in CPI from month before last general pay increase to the base month preceding such base month *if such preceding base month was subsequent to the month before such general pay increase*. (If no such preceding base month, no increase is applicable.)
   2. Payments for months after second month after base month—increase in CPI from month before last general pay increase to base month (regardless of whether other base months intervened).
   3. Payments for months after second month after first base month after retirement—increase in CPI from base month previous to retirement to such first base month.

B. *First Month of Retirement Immediately Preceded by (or Concurrent with) General Pay Increase—Previous Base Month at Least Four Months Previous*
   1. Payments for months before third month after next base month after retirement—no increase is applicable.
   2. Payments for months after second month after next base month after retirement and before third month after the next following base month—increase in CPI from month before such general pay increase to such next base month.
   3. Payments for months after second month after second base month after retirement—increase in CPI from first base month after retirement to next base month.

C. *First Month of Retirement Immediately Preceded by (or Concurrent with) General Pay Increase—Previous Base Month Less than Four Months Previous**
   1. Payments for months before third month after previous base month—no increase is applicable.
   2. Payments for months after second month after previous base month and before third month after next base month—no increase is applicable.
   3. Payments for months after second month after first base month after retirement—increase in CPI from base month previous to retirement to such first base month.

Note: Case when first month of retirement is concurrent with general pay increase *and* with base month falls in category A.

Note: Under a special provision, the payment will not be less than it would have been if the month of retirement had been the month before the month of the general pay increase immediately preceding retirement.

* Up to and including concurrent with month before general pay increase.

crease base month immediately preceding the month of retirement. An adjustment is effective upon retirement after a cost-of-living increase only if there was no pay increase after the prior cost-of-living adjustment. This refined procedure eliminates the abrupt cutoff effect that is present under CSR (and, to some extent, under FEC), as will next be described.

Under CSR, however, there is not such a logical and equitable basis for the first automatic adjustment. Instead, any person on the roll whose effective date of retirement was on or before the first day of the effective month of the increase receives the full amount thereof. In other words, those who retire immediately before an increase get its full advantage even though they were on the payroll while the CPI was rising enough to justify the increase. Such individuals likely received higher pay during at least some of the time because of the rising prices, and also received a larger pension because their average salary is based on a more recent, higher scale. This procedure has been adversely criticized by the General Accounting Office.[10]

A simple solution to this situation would be to prorate the percentage increase according to the proportion of the time after the effective month of the previous automatic adjustment that the individual was on the benefit roll. For example, if an automatic adjustment were made for March 1977 and the next one is 3.4 percent for September 1977, then a person who retires effective in June would receive a 1.7 percent adjustment.

The FEC system handles this problem of the appropriateness of the first adjustment after entry on the roll by another approach. There is a delay of at least a year after the date of injury for which benefits were awarded before a cost-of-living increase can occur.

Table 6 shows the several increases in pension in CSR and the military retirement system as a result of the automatics.

Introduction of 1 Percent Add-On into Automatic Adjustment of Federal Employee Retirement Benefits

In 1969, legislation was enacted that changed the automatic-adjustment provisions of CSR so as to make any triggered increase

---

[10] *Cost-of-Living Adjustment Processes for Federal Annuities Need to be Changed,* Report to the Congress by the Comptroller General of the United States, General Accounting Office, July 27, 1976 and *Cost-of-Living Adjustments for New Federal Retirees: More Rational and Less Costly Processes Are Needed,* Report to the Congress by the Comptroller General of the United States, General Accounting Office, November 17, 1977.

TABLE 6
Effective Months of Automatic Cost-of-Living Increases under Civil Service Retirement and Military Retirement Systems

	Increase	
Effective Month	*CSR*	*Military**
December 1965	6.1%†	4.4%‡
January 1967.................	3.9	3.7
May 1968....................	3.9	3.9
March 1969	3.9	4.0
November 1969	5.0§	5.3§
August 1970	5.6	5.6
June 1971	4.5	4.5
July 1972	4.8	4.8
July 1973	6.1	6.1
January 1974.................	5.5	5.5
July 1974	6.3	6.3
January 1975.................	7.3	7.3
August 1975	5.1	5.1
March 1976	5.4	5.4
March 1977	4.8‖	4.8‖
September 1977	4.3	4.3
March 1978	2.4	2.4

* The month in which the increase occurs was three months earlier for the first increase and one month earlier for each of the next two increases.

† This increase, the first one under the automatic-adjustment provisions, was based on the sum of (1) the CPI increase from calendar year 1962 to September 1965 and (2) 1.5 percent; the latter factor could be said to allow approximately for the situation if the CPI had been taken as a monthly figure at the beginning of 1962, instead of an annual one.

‡ The first automatic adjustment for the military retirement system was for September 1965 (based on the increase in the CPI from calendar year 1962 to August 1965).

§ First increase that included the 1 percent add-on.

‖ First increase on the revised basis after the 1 percent add-on was eliminated.

one percentage point higher than the CPI rise (Public Law 91-93). In other words, if the CPI increased by 3.3 percent from the prior base month to the current one, the benefit increase would be 4.3 percent. Such procedure was adopted shortly afterward by the military retirement system except with respect to the partial adjustment that is made in the initial pension payable (Public Law 91-179) and by the various other retirement systems for federal employees which had the automatic-adjustment feature, but not by FEC (see Table 4). This 1 percent add-on is frequently referred to as the "kicker."

The reason cited for introducing the 1 percent add-on was indeed an interesting example of the political process. In the House of

Representatives, it was argued that this was desirable for the following reason:

> A period of 5 months elapses between the initial month in which the Consumer Price Index rises by 3 percent over the previous base month and the month in which the cost-of-living adjustment is reflected in the annuity checks. During that elapsed period the Consumer Price Index continues its upward trend, generally attaining a level in excess of 1 percent of the actual percentage rate of adjustment. In order to correct this serious deficiency in the adjustment formula and thereby compensate retirees and survivor annuitants for the intervening incremental rises in the cost of living, H.R. 17682 will add 1 percent to all future percentage adjustments.[11]

The error in this reasoning was that such a 1 percent increase would be necessary only for the first adjustment following retirement, and not for all subsequent adjustments. When this logic was pointed out in the Senate consideration of the bill, the proponents did not change the procedure, but rather the rationale! Specifically, in the Senate, the justification for the 1 percent add-on was as follows:

> In order to take into account the increased productivity of a national economy, as well as the possible inaccuracy of the Consumer Price Index as an indicator of purchased goods, particularly for retired employees, the committee approves the addition of a 1-percent adjustment with each cost-of-living increase.[12]

As shown by Table 6, the 1 percent add-on was given ten times from November 1969, when it was first applicable, to March 1976. Because of the compounding effect, this resulted in significantly more than an extra 10 percent. Specifically, the increase in benefits for a pensioner on the roll in October 1969 was 71.7 percent through March 1976 including the effect of the 1 percent add-on, but it would have been only 56.2 percent without it.

Introduction of Notch Provision in Federal Employee Retirement Benefits

The CSR and military retirement systems, as originally constituted, involved inequitable situations with respect to persons retir-

---

[11] *House Report No. 91-158,* April 23, 1969, p. 16.
[12] *Senate Report No. 91-339,* August 1, 1969, p. 5.

ing just after the effective date of an automatic increase as against persons retiring just before such date. Specifically, an individual who retired just before the effective date received the full increase (of 3 percent or more), while the one with a similar employment history who retired just afterwards did not, and the slightly higher annuity (due to additional service and possibly higher average salary) was almost always insufficient to offset the loss of the CPI adjustment.

This situation was magnified in the early 1970s with respect to top-level civil service employees with long service. Their salaries had been literally frozen (at about the $35,000–38,000 range) during this period, despite the rises in the general levels of salaries and prices, because they were tied to the salary of Members of Congress, which had not then been increased directly.[13] As a result, such individuals would tend to have a *smaller* annuity the longer they worked, since if they had retired earlier the basic initial amount would have been about the same (only slightly shorter length of service but the same average three-year salary), but there would have been added, over the years, the substantial increases due to the automatic adjustments (including the 1 percent add-on). See Table 6.[14]

Accordingly, a "notch" (or "smooth-junction") provision was urgently needed. Such a provision was enacted for both CSR (Public Law 93-136, 1973) and the military retirement system (Public Law 13-110, 1973). It provides that the initial pension amount shall not be less than what it would have been if the retiree had become entitled to pension on the day before the effective month of the automatic adjustment occurring just prior to retirement (and also for the military retirement plan, not less than the retired pay to which the retiree would have become entitled on retirement on the day before the effective date of the pay rates on which the retired pay is based).

This notch provision was a long step toward providing an equitable smooth junction for retirements at slightly different dates.

---

[13] Congressional remuneration was increased, at times, by changes in allowances for expenses related to the carrying out of the duties of the office.

[14] This inequitable situation was "avoided," within the letter of the law, by such persons retiring and then returning to the same job as a "rehired annuitant" (with pay equal to normal salary minus CSR annuity) or as an "independent contractor" (with both CSR annuity and, in essence, full pay).

However, it still left an inequitable, illogical situation for high-level civil service employees with frozen (or virtually frozen) salaries. Although the pension amount as computed as of the retirement date would be increased to the higher amount that it would have been for retirement just before the last previous automatic increase, it still might be less than the pension amount for retirement just before the second (or even earlier) prior automatic increase. It would be a simple technical matter to amend the law to take into account this possibility.

Elimination of 1 Percent Add-On from Automatic Adjustment of Federal Employee Retirement Benefits

The unusual, illogical, 1 percent add-on feature was subject to adverse criticism from its very inception. This was due at least in part to the underlying logic for it having been "switched in the middle of the stream." Then, as inflation heightened in 1973–75 and the add-on was more frequently given, further criticism arose about this far-more-favorable treatment of federal employees than was applicable for other classes of retirees in the nation.

In the forefront of those in the battle to repeal the 1 percent add-on was former Congressman Hastings Keith, who himself was a beneficiary of this windfall. He published articles on the subject in the *Wall Street Journal* (August 25, 1976) and in *Readers Digest* (September 1976). Other criticisms of this provision appeared in such diverse publications as *New Republic* (August 7 and 14, 1976), *Pensions* (July 1976), and *Playboy* (November 1976), as well as in many newspaper editorials. The National Taxpayers Union, Washington, D.C., placed full-page ads attacking the 1 percent add-on in several prominent newspapers (e.g., the *Wall Street Journal* for May 27, 1976).

A number of these criticisms used calculations made by the author (who also was a beneficiary of this provision) as to its long-range cost effect for CSR and the military pension system combined under several assumed sets of future economic conditions. Specifically, it was estimated that through 1975 the 1 percent kicker had already resulted in an additional $1 billion of cost and that the past increases would result in future costs of about $13 billion. It was also estimated that with price inflation of 6 percent per year, the increased pension outgo in the future for present pensioners and their surviving spouses because of such inflation would be $84 billion. The corresponding figure on the basis of annual price inflation of 12 percent was $389 billion; analyses at such an extreme assumption were made at the time legislative change was being urged, in part at least because inflation was running at this level at times during 1974–75.

Quite naturally, various federal employee groups were strongly opposed to the elimination of the 1 percent add-on. In its defense, the argument was put forward that it was necessary in order to allow for the lag in making the adjustments as against the actual continuous monthly rises in the CPI.[15] Also, the argument for "sharing in the increased productivity of the nation," as used by the Senate when the legislation was enacted, was repeated (although during 1974–75, productivity changes seemed to be negative).

Some recommended going even further than eliminating the 1 percent kicker. They proposed that pension amounts which had been increased by the add-on should be frozen until future increases due to CPI changes had compensated for its past effect.[16] From a political approach, such a procedure was scarcely feasible.

The Ford Administration, as well as a number of members of Congress with responsibility in this area (including Representative David N. Henderson, Chairman of the House Post Office and Civil Service Committee), and the General Accounting Office[17] also entered the fray and made various proposals to eliminate the 1 percent add-on. In some instances, a "sweetener" was added to this proposal, such as by having a 3 percent increase in the CPI immediately trigger the automatic adjustment in the first month that such increase occurs, rather than requiring it to be maintained for three

---

[15] This point was made in the report "Postretirement Adjustment of Military and Federal Civil Service Retired Pay," prepared by E. J. Devine and Marcella L. Wojdylak, Appendix H of *Interim Report to the President and the Congress,* Defense Manpower Commission, May 16, 1975. In fact, here it was argued (illogically, in the author's opinion) that continuous monthly adjustment is desirable and proper, even though it can be obtained only by approximate retrospective methods.

[16] This was proposed, for example, in a bill introduced in April 1976 by Representative Paul Findley (H.R. 13335).

[17] See "Cost-of-Living Adjustment Processes for Federal Annuities Need to be Changed," *Report to the Congress by the Comptroller General of the United States,* July 27, 1976. This report also criticized the payment of full cost-of-living increases under CSR to those retiring shortly before the effective date of an increase and recommended instead pro rata increase payments.

successive months or by shortening the period from the base month to the effective month of the pension increase. For example, Representative Henderson introduced H.R. 14520 in June 1976 (which was similar to an earlier bill, H.R. 3310) that would trigger the increase the first month that the CPI rose by at least 3 percent, and then the increase would be paid two months after the end of such month (as compared with three months under existing law). The Ford Administration proposal was less generous; it would only have eliminated the 1 percent add-on and would have left unchanged the three-month measuring period for the trigger and the three-month period thereafter before the increase showed up in the pension check.

The actual legislative procedure in repealing the 1 percent add-on was complicated by the fact that this provision was incorporated into a number of federal retirement systems, and these were under the jurisdiction of different congressional committees. Accordingly, it was a question of timing as to who should act first, and then would do so.

Legislation was enacted in mid-1976 that repealed the 1 percent add-on for the Foreign Service Retirement system and the military retirement system, but this was contingent on its being done also for CSR.[18] The House Civil Service Committee was hesitant about taking this action (probably because of the close relations of many of its members with federal-employee groups). Finally, Representative Henderson sought to bypass much of the legislative snarl by bringing his bill onto the floor of the House under the "suspension of rules" procedure. This was done on August 2, 1976. Although the vote was favorable, by 238 to 143, the proposal was defeated because a two-thirds majority is required under such procedure.

This defeat, coming so late in the session, seemed to doom the possible repeal of the 1 percent add-on in 1976, and several statements to this effect were made by congressional leaders. However, in September 1976, as a result of an unexpected move by Senators Ernest F. Hollings and Lawton Chiles, an amendment repealing the 1 percent add-on in CSR, the Foreign Service Retirement system, and the military retirement system was added on the floor of the Senate to a bill making appropriations for the legislative branch.

---

[18] This was done in Public Law 94-350 (July 12, 1976) for the Foreign Service Retirement system and in Public Law 94-361 (July 14, 1976) for the military retirement system.

This amendment was accepted by the conference committee between the House and the Senate, and the bill was signed into law by President Ford on October 1, 1976 (Public Law 94-440).

Present Automatic-Adjustment Provisions for Federal Retirement Benefits

The new automatic-adjustment provisions eliminating the 1 percent add-on apply not only to CSR, the Foreign Service Retirement system, and the military retirement system, but also to the plans for the Central Intelligence Agency (which uses whatever procedure is followed by the military retirement system) and for the plan of the Board of Governors of the Federal Reserve System and the Former Lighthouse Service (both of which are tied to the CSR procedure). No change in such provisions for the several District of Columbia plans (for teachers and judges and for survivor benefits for fire fighters and police) was made by this hasty 1976 legislation. However, the necessary legislative action to remove the 1 percent add-on in those plans was being given quite active consideration in mid-1978 (in H.R. 6536, which has the primary purpose of establishing these plans on an actuarially sound financing basis, and which the House had passed, and there seemed every likelihood of similar action by the Senate).

The new provisions are quite simple and are reasonably logical and equitable. The adjustments are to be made semiannually, regardless of the size of the increase in the CPI (but not in the event of a decrease). The base months are each June and December. Each March the increase from the previous June to the previous December (rounded to the nearest 0.1 percent) is applied to the pension amount for February[19] in order to determine the pension for that month and thereafter. The same procedure is followed each September—based on the increase in the CPI from the previous December to the previous June. For the first such adjustment—that for March 1977—the increase in the CPI was prescribed by the legislation to be measured from December 1975 (the last effective base month under the previous procedure) to December 1976 (see Table 6).

---

[19] Or, for a pension with a commencing date of March 1, to the initially computed pension amount.

As long as the CPI rises steadily, the new provision will work out quite reasonably and equitably. However, if the CPI fluctuates both upward and downward—as it has at times in the past, although currently little expectation of this exists—an anomaly will arise.

Let us suppose that for a particular June the CPI is 200, that it increases by 3 percent (to 206) for the next December, that it then decreases to 200 for the next June, that it then increases back to 206 for the next December, and so forth, on into the future. What would then happen—despite the fact that the CPI is, on the whole, remaining relatively level—is that annuity amounts would increase by 3 percent each December, remaining unchanged after each June consideration. Quite obviously, this is illogical and unreasonable to have the annuity continually increase each year even though prices, in essence, remain stable.

The simple solution would be to base the adjustment on the preceding sixth months unless it had not triggered a benefit increase, in which case the last previous trigger month would be used. Specifically, for example, if for June of a particular year no increase resulted because the CPI for that month was lower than that for the preceding December (which had triggered an increase), then the comparison for the following December would be with the preceding December and not with the preceding June.

In the actual future experience, if inflation slows down considerably, it may be found that another change should be made. It would hardly be worthwhile, from a policy standpoint or administratively, to make semiannual adjustments of the order of 1 percent or less. Thus, for example, a minimum increase of 2 percent over the last previous base month might be introduced as a requirement.

One survivor benefit system for federal civilian employees, namely, that for the federal judiciary, was not indexed after the pensioner had entered on the rolls until recently, although it was very adequately indexed before the death of the member, whether before or after retirement. The survivor benefits were based on the average salary during the five years before the death of the judge (retired judges continue to receive salary, and this is counted just as for active judges) and on the years of service (including those as a retired judge). However, once the survivor benefit had started, it remained fixed thereafter.

In 1976, Public Law 94-554 introduced a unique indexing method for the judicial survivor annuity system (at the same time reducing the five-year averaging period for salaries to a three-year one). Each time that judicial salaries are increased, for each 5 percent rise in salary of the category of judge in which the deceased had served will produce a 3 percent increase in the survivor pension.

This provision—strangely enough in a plan developed for the highest level of judges in the country—is very poorly designed. An increase in judicial salaries of less than 5 percent will have no effect on the survivor benefits since it is not carried over to the next determination when another salary increase occurs. Thus, for example, if there are two successive salary increases of 4 percent each, no change will occur in the survivor annuities. However, if these salary increases had been 2 percent and 6 percent, respectively—thus producing virtually the same eventual pay—the survivor annuities would be increased 3 percent.

INDEXING PROVISIONS IN OTHER FEDERAL PROGRAMS

Automatic-adjustment provisions have been adopted in a number of federal programs in addition to those providing periodic benefits for government employees. Perhaps the most important of these are the Supplemental Security Income (SSI) and food stamp programs.

SSI (which is one of the titles of the Social Security Act and is administered by the Social Security Administration) is, in essence, a guaranteed income program for persons aged 65 and over, for the permanently and totally disabled, and for the blind.[20] It is completely federally financed (from general revenues), and it replaced the previous public assistance programs for these categories,[21] which were administered by the states and jointly financed by the federal government and the states. SSI was enacted in October 1972 (in Public Law 92-603, as part of the Social Security Amendments of 1972), to be effective in January 1974.

---

[20] For more details on the SSI program, see Robert J. Myers, *Social Security* (Homewood, Ill.: Richard D. Irwin, Inc., 1975), pp. 413–19.

[21] The states can have programs supplementing SSI. In some instances, they must do so, in order to maintain the level of payments under the previous public assistance programs.

Initially, the SSI payment amounts were legislated to be on a flat, fixed basis, although an ad hoc increase was enacted before the program became effective, and another one was so provided for July 1974.[22] However, legislation in August 1974 (Public Law 93-368) incorporated the same type of automatic-adjustment procedure for SSI as is used for the OASDI system (such principle having been originally legislated in July 1972, before SSI was enacted). As a result of the automatic-adjustment provisions, the SSI basic amount increased by 8.0 percent (from $146.00 to $157.70) for June 1975 by 6.4 percent (to $167.80) for June 1976, by 5.9 percent (to $177.80) for June 1977, and by 6.5 percent (to $189.40) for June 1978.

The food stamp program, which is really an income supplementation device rather than a plan to provide more nutritious diets or to distribute surplus foods, makes payments to persons with low incomes.[23] The individual or family may purchase a prescribed amount of food stamps (which are equivalent to money when buying groceries) at a reduced price. The reduction thus represents the federal payment. The total amount of food stamps (both purchased and "free") per month varies by family size and is adjusted automatically every six months on the basis of changes in the food component in the CPI. The change effective for January is based on the movement in the CPI from the previous February to the previous August, while that for July is based on the August–February movement. Unlike the automatics under OASDI, there can be downward movements as well as upward ones. Within certain limits, the proportion of the food stamps which must be purchased can be varied by the Secretary of Agriculture.

Benefits under the child nutrition (school lunch) and elderly nutrition (subsidized group meals) programs are subject to automatic adjustment, by the food-away-from-home component of the CPI. Under the former, the adjustments are effective semiannually (January and July) and are based on May–November changes. Under the latter, the adjustments are effective annually (July) and are based on May–May changes.

---

[22] The basic amount (which is reduced by other income—or under some circumstances, a portion of other income) was $130 per month initially for a single person, and 50 percent more for an eligible couple. The amount was increased to $140 effective January 1974 and to $146 effective July 1974.

[23] For more details on the food stamp program, see Robert J. Myers, *Social Security* (Homewood, Ill.: Richard D. Irwin, Inc., 1975), pp. 407–13.

The so-called "black lung" program for disabled miners (pneumoconiosis), which was established by federal law in 1969, has built-in automatic-adjustment provisions of the "current pay for grade at which retired" type. The basic benefit rate (before supplements for dependents) is established at 50 percent of the current FEC benefit for total disability for a federal employee at the entrance salary of grade GS-2 (i.e., General Service 2). The choice of this grade, which is applicable in practice for only the least skilled and experienced of clerical workers, was purely arbitrary.

STATE WORKERS' COMPENSATION PROGRAM

The workers' compensation system in the United States (WC) provides economic security in case of work-connected accidents or diseases. It is based on separate programs in each state, the District of Columbia, and outlying areas such as Puerto Rico (plus the Federal Employees Compensation, longshoremen's and harbor workers', and black lung programs, as discussed previously in this chapter). Indexing provisions are present in a number of these programs with respect to two elements. As is generally the case about state-administered programs, as compared with nationwide programs, accurate information in summary form is difficult to obtain. Accordingly, the material presented here, although believed to be correct, may not be fully complete.[24]

One element that is indexed is the maximum weekly payment as it relates to initial claims. Such element for the worker alone (some states add dependents benefits thereto) is indexed in the programs of 38 states and the District of Columbia (as of January 1, 1978) for changes in the statewide average weekly wage, with the indexing being done on an annual basis, except in two states (Illinois does so semiannually, while Maine does so biennially). The National Commission on State Workmen's Compensation Laws, which was established by Congress under the Occupational Safety and Health Act of 1970, made the "essential" recommenda-

---

[24] For a summary of the provisions of these programs, see *Analysis of Workers' Compensation Laws, 1978 Edition* (Washington, D.C.: Chamber of Commerce of the United States, January 1, 1978). This publication, however, gives only limited information about escalation of benefits (particularly those in course of payment). More detailed information was obtained from *Workers' Compensation Escalating Benefits* (Menlo Park, Calif.: Argonaut Insurance Co., June 1977); and from the National Council on Compensation Insurance, New York, N.Y.

tion that all state programs should follow this procedure.[25] The commission pointed out that in 1972, only 13 state programs had such flexible maximums.[26]

The other element that is indexed is the amount of the periodic benefit after it has been in course of payment for some time. The National Commission on State Workmen's Compensation Laws made an "other than essential" recommendation that beneficiaries in permanent total disability cases and in death cases should have their benefits adjusted in proportion to increases in statewide average weekly wages.[27] It should be noted that this recommended basis is, under normal circumstances, a more liberal one than if it were based on changes in the CPI.

In some instances, benefits in course of payment are increased to recognize changes in wage levels only for those affected by the maximum-benefit provision. This can happen in either of two ways in some (but by no means all) state systems. The maximum benefit is generally a certain percentage of the statewide average weekly wage (SAWW). In some instances, the percentage may be increased, and persons previously receiving a benefit held down by the maximum will receive an increase whereas other beneficiaries will not. In other instances, when the SAWW increases, the same thing can occur. Or else both can occur simultaneously.

As an example of the foregoing situation, in Alaska the maximum benefit rates are the following percentages of the SAWW: 80 percent in 1975, 100 percent in 1976, 133⅓ percent in 1977–78, 166⅔ percent in 1979–80, and 200 percent in 1981 and after. The individual's benefit rate is 66⅔ percent of his or her average weekly wage (as a result, for example, ultimately only those with wages in excess of three times the SAWW will be affected by the maximum-benefit provision). As both the percentage of SAWW used in determining the maximum benefit and the SAWW rise, persons on the benefit roll affected by the maximum receive increases (but not those whose benefits were originally below the maximum, or those whose benefits later become below the increasing maximum). In other words, the individual's benefit of 66⅔ percent of his or

[25] *The Report of the National Commission on State Workmen's Compensation* (Washington, D.C.: U.S. Government Printing Office, July 1972), p. 64.

[26] See the commission's report *Compendium on Workmen's Compensation* (Washington, D.C.: U.S. Government Printing Office, 1973) p. 117.

[27] See pages 64 and 71 of its report (referred to in footnote 25).

her average weekly wage is not indexed over time but rather only the maximum-benefit limitation is escalated.

Michigan provides automatic increases for benefits in course of payment for only a very limited category of extremely permanently and totally disabled cases (involving loss, or loss of use, of two or more major members—hands, feet, and eyes—or general paralysis or insanity). The maximum weekly benefit for new cases is automatically changed each year for increases in the SAWW, and the minimum weekly benefit is changed by the same dollar amount (now resulting in a spread of only $37 between the minimum and the maximum). Persons in the foregoing category receive 66⅔ percent of their average weekly wage, but adjusted from time to time to reflect the changing minimum and maximum benefit amounts. Thus, for a case of long duration, the maximum, even though rising, might prevail for some years; then the benefit would be level at 66⅔ percent of the individual's past actual average wage, and then it would rise at the level of the increasing minimum benefit.

It is notable that the programs of ten states (Connecticut, Florida, Idaho, Illinois, Maine, Minnesota, New Hampshire, Oregon, Vermont, and Virginia) and the District of Columbia automatically increase all benefits of a particular category which are in payment status for changes in economic conditions. This is also done under the U.S. Longshoremen's and Harbor Workers' Compensation Act, which has identical provisions with the District of Columbia program. All adjustments are made annually (beginning January in some cases and in July or October in others). Connecticut was the first state to adopt such escalation (in 1966). The other programs generally did so in 1972 or later.

WC benefits are generally classified into one of five different types—temporary partial disability, temporary total disability, permanent partial disability, permanent total disability, and death (or survivor). All of the 11 systems index the permanent total disability benefits, but this is not always done for the other benefits. All escalate the death benefits except Connecticut, Florida, Idaho, New Hampshire, and Vermont. The District of Columbia system does not do so when the death occurs as a result of causes unrelated to the work-connected injury or disease.

Six states—Connecticut, Idaho, Maine, Oregon, Vermont, and Virginia—escalate the temporary total disability benefits. Only a few states appear to apply automatic adjustments to partial disability benefits (undoubtedly because it would be very difficult to do this for this type of benefit). New Hampshire does not escalate its WC benefits when the individual is receiving social security disability benefits. Virginia does not do so if the combined WC and social security disability benefits are 80 percent or more of previous wage (which would seem to create a "notch" problem as between cases just under and just over this boundary).

The method of escalation in the District of Columbia system and in all others except Connecticut, Florida, Idaho, and Virginia is based on the percentage change in the SAWW over some past period of time. All such programs make automatic adjustments without any maximum limit, except Minnesota, which in 1977 instituted an annual maximum increase of 6 percent (noncumulative).

As an example of how indexing of benefits in course of payment is done, let us consider the District of Columbia system where escalation is effective on October 1 of each year. It is determined from the increase in the average weekly wage of all production or nonsupervisory workers in private nonagricultural employment in the nation (rather than just the geographical area of D.C.) for the nine-month period ending on the previous June 30 over such average wage for the nine-month period ending on the second previous June 30. The data are obtained from surveys conducted by the Bureau of Labor Statistics, U.S. Department of Labor (as released in its publication, *Employment and Earnings,* Chart C-1). The escalation is done for only permanent and total disability cases, and not for temporary disability cases, and for survivor benefits where the death was due to the work-connected cause of injury or disease. Under these circumstances, the increases are logically based on the change in the nationwide average wage from the date of disablement, rather than from the date of determining that the disability is "permanent" (so that no difference occurs depending upon when such administrative action is taken), although the increase in the benefit is payable only prospectively (from the latter date).

Connecticut and Idaho increase WC benefits in payment status by flat weekly amounts—namely, the dollar amount obtained by multiplying the maximum dollar benefit by the percentage increase in the SAWW. This procedure, of course, provides greater relative increases than that in the SAWW for beneficiaries at payment levels below the maximum (although usually a high proportion of the beneficiaries are at the maximum).

Florida provides uniform increases in all benefits of 5 percent of the original benefit amount (i.e., on a noncompounded basis) each January 1 following the date of disablement. This, as occurs also in other ways under other WC programs, creates a "notch" situation as between persons with virtually identical circumstances who become disabled at slightly different times.

Virginia is the only state to use the CPI for purposes of automatic adjustment of WC benefits in course of payment. Such increases are effective on each October 1 and are based on the increase in the nationwide CPI for the preceding calendar year over that for the second preceding calendar year.

The escalator provisions of the various WC programs are financed in two ways. In all systems except Florida and Illinois (and Oregon as to permanent disability and death cases), the financing for each individual case is provided through the insurance carrier (i.e., by the employer in the premium structure, or directly when self-insurance is done). The other basis is to assess all carriers (and self-insured employers) on a uniform percentage basis relative to their premium charges, regardless of the actual beneficiaries on the roll arising from the employment of the particular employer.

Some members of Congress in recent years have taken the position that the states have been too slow in implementing the recommendations of the National Commission and have introduced federal legislation to liberalize WC benefits (on the other hand, other persons believe that state laws have been moving rapidly to meet the recommendations). The mechanism in the initial bill introduced (S. 2008, by Senators Williams and Javits in 1973) would be to apply the provisions of the Longshoremen's and Harborworkers' Compensation Act (i.e., the District of Columbia system) in all states that do not meet the benefit standards prescribed in the legislation.

A later bill (S. 2018, by Senators Williams, Javits, and others in 1975) instead would apply the benefit standards in the bill in all states with less liberal provisions. Under this bill, the benefits would have to be "adjusted, at least annually, to reflect increases in the statewide average weekly wage." This provision is not entirely precise because it is not clear whether "reflect" means complete recognition of any relative change of the SAWW or only a fraction of it. Nor was the bill clear as to which types of benefits would be subject to adjustment.

A bill introduced in 1977 by Representative Gaydos (H.R. 2058) follows the same procedure, except that it provides for an 8 percent maximum on the annual increases (apparently on a noncumulative basis) and clearly applies only to permanent and total disability cases and to survivor benefits. In the author's opinion, increases in WC benefits in course of payment should equitably be made on the basis of changes in the CPI, rather than by changes in wage levels (which would likely produce larger increases).

Indexing of Benefits of State and Local Employee Retirement Systems in the United States

Because there are well over 6,000 retirement systems for state and local government employees in the United States, it is impossible to give a detailed discussion and analysis of their provisions for indexing retirement benefits. The following comments and analyses are based on data developed by various organizations and persons in broader studies of state and local retirement plans, namely, the National Association of State Retirement Administrators; the Labor-Management Relations Service of the National League of Cities, the United States Conference of Mayors, the National Association of Counties; the National Education Association; Hay-Huggins, Inc.; and Robert Tilove, senior vice president, Martin E. Segal Company.

In the past decade, there has been a rapidly growing trend for state and local retirement systems to make some provisions for increasing pension benefits for those on the roll, often under automatic-adjustment procedures. This has been especially true for large systems, such as statewide ones. Such a movement occurred because of the relatively large price increases taking place and because of the precedent of such provisions being adopted in 1962 by the federal government for CSR and the military retirement system.

Two state and local retirement plans had automatic-adjustment features previous to 1962, but they were routine or guaranteed and were not linked to changes in the CPI. Instead, they provided increases of a small percentage on a routine or guaranteed basis. As a result, the pension amounts were expected to keep more or less up to date with a low rate of inflation, such as had been prevalent for a number of years following the Korean conflict in the early 1950s.[1]

INDEXING PROVISIONS OF LARGE STATE AND LOCAL RETIREMENT PLANS IN 1972

Robert Tilove made a broad survey of 129 of the largest state and local retirement systems as of the beginning of 1972.[2] The plans represented less than 5 percent of all such plans then in existence, but included about 70 percent of all persons covered by such plans. He found that 26 of the 51 state plans for general employees (with 2.4 million employees) had some type of adjustment provision—5 with routine automatic percentage increases, independent of CPI changes (ranging from 1 percent to 2 percent generally), 12 with automatics based on the CPI (6 with maximums of less than 3 percent), 1 based on salary changes, and 8 of other types. In the 31 local plans for general employees, 15 plans (with 277,000 employees) had adjustment provisions—5 with routine automatics (mostly with 2 percent maximums), 7 with CPI automatics (mostly with 3 percent or higher maximums, or none at all), and 3 of other types. The 70 retirement systems for teachers included 33 plans with adjustment provisions (2.2 million employees)—10 with routine automatics (generally less than 3 percent), 12 with CPI automatics (4 with maximums of 1 percent but less than 2 percent, and the remainder with maximums of 3 percent or more).

CURRENT INDEXING PROVISIONS IN STATEWIDE RETIREMENT PLANS

Table 7 presents information about the provisions for adjusting pension benefits for the major general statewide retirement systems

---

[1] This was done first in the Chicago system for school teachers in 1959 and later in other Illinois plans and then in Hawaii in 1961 and Nevada in 1963; the first automatic-adjustment provision involving changes in the CPI was adopted by Massachusetts in 1966. (See John P. Mackin, "Protecting Purchasing Power in Retirement" [New York: Fleet Academic Editions, Inc., 1971], pp. 126–30.)

[2] Robert Tilove, *Public Employee Pension Funds* (New York: Columbia University Press, 1976), p. 44.

TABLE 7
Postretirement Adjustments to Pension Benefits in Major General State Retirement Systems

State	Adjustments	State	Adjustments
Alabama	No automatic adjustments; ad hoc adjustments made from time to time; latest of 15% in 1973.	Massachusetts	Automatic adjustment up or down when CPI changes by 3% or more; 1969 payments considered as floor.
Alaska	Cost-of-living allowance of 25% of social security payable to retirants living in Alaska.	Michigan	No provision for automatic adjustment.
Arizona	No automatic adjustments.	Minnesota	No cost-of-living adjustments; benefits subject to annual adjustment depending upon investment income and market value of stocks.
Arkansas	Maximum of ½ of 1% annually, if CPI has increased by that amount.		
California	Automatic adjustments based on CPI but limited to 2% annually.	Mississippi	Annual supplement of 1½% times number of years retired.
Colorado	Automatic increases of 3% annually.	Missouri	No provision.
Connecticut	Automatic annual adjustments tied to CPI; increases may vary within range of 1–3%; June 1973 pension regarded as floor.	Montana	Ad hoc adjustment made for those retiring before 1971, updated to 1973.
		Nebraska	None reported.‖
Delaware	No automatic increases.	Nevada	Automatic annual increase of 1.5% of original allowance.
Florida	Automatic cost-of-living adjustment not to exceed 3% annually.	New Hampshire	No automatic adjustment, change by ad hoc legislation only.
Georgia	Automatic cost-of-living adjustment not to exceed 3% annually.	New Jersey	Automatic adjustments (after 3-year waiting period) based on one half the rise in CPI.
Hawaii	Automatic increases of 2½% annually.		
Idaho	Board may authorize adjustments up to 3% annually, under certain conditions.	New Mexico	No automatic adjustment; special adjustments made on ad hoc basis for annuitants retired prior to 1970.
Illinois	Automatic annual increases of 2%.	New York	Automatic cost-of-living increases based on CPI on first $8,000 of pension to those over 62 years of age.*
Indiana	None.		
Iowa	Ad hoc increase of 8.276% for retirees effective 7/1/73.		
Kansas	Increase granted beginning 7/1/73 for those retired before 1/1/71.	North Carolina	Automatic increases ranging from 1 to 4% of CPI based on degree of rise in CPI.†
Kentucky	None.	North Dakota	None.
Louisiana	Increases based on CPI not to exceed 3% annually.	Ohio	Automatic increase of 1½% (after 3 years) applies each year CPI rises that much.
Maine	Automatic increases based on percentage increase received by active employees in general salary adjustments.	Oklahoma	None.
		Oregon	Special supplements granted to retirees effective 1/1/74; effective 7/1/73, annual cost-of-living adjustments limited to 2%.
Maryland	Automatic adjustments annually based on CPI.		

TABLE 7 (continued)

State	Adjustments	State	Adjustments
Pennsylvania	No automatic adjustments; legislature has from time to time provided supplemental and minimum allowances to retired members, generally based on change in CPI since retirement.		1½% increase is automatically granted provided CPI indicates such change is warranted.
		Vermont	Annual adjustments related to CPI within limits of 1 to 3%.
Rhode Island	Automatic increases of 3% (after 3 years retirement) not compounded (different factor for pre-1968 retirees).	Virginia	Automatic cost-of-living adjustment related to CPI every two years; changes in benefit formula also apply to retirees.
		Washington	None reported.§
South Carolina	No automatic adjustments; supplemental allowance granted.‡	West Virginia	No provision for automatic adjustment.
South Dakota	None.	Wisconsin	Adjustments prohibited by constitution; but annuities can be increased by use of surplus in annuity reserve account.
Tennessee	None.		
Texas	No automatic adjustments; legislature granted seven increases in postwar period through 1973.		
		Wyoming	No automatic adjustments; various ad hoc increases have been granted since 1961.
Utah	7½% cost-of-living increase given retired members after 5 years; thereafter, an annual		

* Based on investigation by the author, this provision is not really automatic (see text).

† Based on investigation by the author, this provision is not really automatic but rather is a contingent provision based on funds available.

‡ Based on investigation by the author, this provision should read: "Automatic adjustments based on CPI of 4% if CPI rises by at least 3%."

§ Based on investigation by the author, this state had a provision similar to that of Idaho (which is discussed in some detail in the text).

‖ Based on investigation by the author, this should be "none."

Reproduced with permission, from *Employee Pension Systems in State and Local Government*, Research Publication No. 33, Tax Foundation, Inc., 1976.

Source: National Association of State Retirement Administrators, Survey of State Retirement Systems, June 30, 1974.

in each of the 50 states as of 1974. A wide diversity of procedures is followed. In 29 states, no automatic adjustments of a definite prescribed nature are provided, although in many of them ad hoc increases are made from time to time and often these are based on changes in the CPI.

The pensions under the Minnesota plan vary with the level of the investment income and the market value of the common stocks held, but the adjustments will never reduce the pension amount below that initially awarded. In other words, this plan follows the variable-annuity approach, and the fluctuating amounts of the pensions will hopefully move with the costs of living, but in practice may not do so (and, in fact, have not done so). The same general situation also prevails in Wisconsin. In Nebraska (a money-purchase plan with an insurance company), dividends based on experience are payable. These three plans cannot be considered as involving "indexing" as the term is used here.

One state, Maine, automatically adjusts pensions in force in accordance with changes in the general salary level of active workers. This is similar to what was done for many years in the military retirement system (but no longer is) and to what is done for the federal judiciary. It is probably the most liberal (and costly) provision of all.

In the other 20 states, there are automatic-adjustment procedures of various types. In five states, the adjustment is completely routine and automatic, being independent of CPI changes; such prescribed increase is on a noncompounded basis of 1½ percent per year in two states and 2, 2½, and 3 percent in the other three states.[3] In the other 15 states, the automatic percentage increase depends on the CPI rising, although in all but 3 states (Maryland, Massachusetts, and Virginia), the increase has limitations of one sort or another, so that it may not equal the full rise in the CPI for all beneficiaries. It is important to note that all indexing procedures based on the CPI (whether or not with maximums) are on a compounded basis, which is more advantageous for the beneficiary than if on a noncompounded, simple interest basis.

In at least two plans, an employee contribution is required to assist in the financing of the automatic increases in pensions in force. In both instances, these plans provide increases on a fully automatic basis, irrespective of changes in the CPI. In Illinois (2 percent simple annual increases), the special additional employee contribution rate is ½ percent, which is refundable without interest upon separation from service before retirement. In Hawaii (3 percent simple annual increases), the special additional employee contribution rate is 1.8 percent.

In New Jersey, the increase in the benefit amount is only half the rise in the CPI; decreases can also occur, but cannot reduce below the original amount. In several states, the first adjustment is de-

---

[3] A 3 percent noncompounded annual basis would, for example, result in a 30 percent increase after ten years, while a 3 percent compounded annual basis would yield a 55.8 percent increase. Further, according to the U.S. Total Males Life Table for 1969–71 at 6 percent interest, the value at age 65 of such a noncompounded-increase life annuity of $100 per month is $11,773, as against $12,208 for one on a compounded-increase basis, the latter being 3.7 percent larger than the former.

ferred for several years after retirement (e.g., for three years in both New Jersey and Rhode Island, and for five years in Utah, but then retroactive by being, at most, 7½ percent at that time and 1½ percent per year thereafter).

In 11 states, the increase in the pension amount as a result of indexing by the CPI is subject to a maximum annual limitation. Generally, any "unrecognized" increase in the CPI in a particular year due to such a maximum can be carried over to succeeding years (for example, under a 3 percent maximum, if the CPI rises 5 percent one year and remains unchanged the next year, the adjustment would be 3 percent for the first year and 2 percent for the next year). This maximum is ½ percent in one state, 1½ percent in two states, 2 percent in one state, 3 percent in six states, and 4 percent in one state (South Carolina, where this increase is given if the CPI rises at least 3 percent, a provision which has some similarity—although by no means complete—to the now-repealed 1 percent add-on under the federal Civil Service Retirement system). Considering the current economic conditions, these plans with maximum limits operate in practice in the same way as do those with completely routine, fixed automatic increases provided.

At the time that the data in Table 7 were published (mid-1974), Idaho and Washington had a unique provision for adjustment of pensions in course of payment, which can be considered to be semiautomatic (but not fully automatic). An adjustment based on the CPI would be made each year, with a maximum of 3 percent, but only if the system were in financial balance (when comparing the required employer contribution rate after the increase with that at the previous valuation). Interestingly, provision was made for possible decreases if the CPI went down, but again with the same 3 percent limit and also with the proviso that the amount could never be reduced below the initial amount at the time of retirement. In 1976, Idaho increased the maximum limitation to 6 percent, and it was further provided that a 1 percent increase would be given (if justified by the CPI change) regardless of the financial status of the plan. In 1974, North Carolina introduced a similar provision to that in the versions of the Idaho and Washington plans then in effect (but with a 4 percent maximum). Alaska added such a provision in 1975.

In 1977, New York inaugurated a unique automatic-adjustment procedure, applicable only to those first entering service after 1976. Before that time, the situation in New York was rather complicated, but it may properly be said that its indexing procedures had not really been automatic; they were ad hoc "temporary" increases beginning in 1968, legislated each year, with routine extension of past "temporary" increases. The new procedure, applicable not only to all state employees—general, teachers, and police and fire fighters (hereafter referred to as "public safety")—but also to all employees of New York City (who have separate retirement systems from state employees) is termed CO-ESC. The "CO" part relates to coordination with social security, while the "ESC" refers to escalation (or indexing of benefits).

Under the New York CO-ESC provisions, except under the plans for public safety employees, those who defer retirement until age 65 have available automatic adjustments based on the CPI, but with a 3 percent maximum increase annually. For earlier retirements, the maximum or cap is proportionately reduced, until indexing is not granted to those retiring at age 62 or before. For example, for retirement at age 63, the indexing is based on a 1 percent maximum annual increase, and for retirement at age 64 on a 2 percent maximum. Public safety employees have the full escalation provision (3 percent annual maximum) for retirement after 25 years of service. Employees retiring before age 65 can defer the start of their pension until age 65 and then receive the full escalation provision (applicable from age 62 on), subject to the 3 percent annual maximum.[4]

Also, following 1974, South Dakota instituted automatic-adjustment provisions based on the CPI (with an annual maximum increase of 3 percent). At the same time, in several states the maximum permissible increase was raised (1½ percent in Arkansas; 2 percent, after two years on the roll, in Ohio; and 5 percent in Vermont).

CURRENT INDEXING PROVISIONS IN MUNICIPAL
RETIREMENT PLANS

Information about postretirement adjustment of pensions by municipal governments is available from three surveys made by the Labor-Management Relations Service of the National League of

---

[4] From an actuarial standpoint, the option to defer receiving retirement pensions so as to have the indexing provision is not a "good buy" because it has about a 10 percent lower value. The availability of the escalation feature does, however, offer inducement to defer retirement (as well as the inducement being present of having the salary in the interim and the larger basic benefit due to more service).

Cities, the United States Conference of Mayors, and the National Association of Counties (with the cosponsorship of the International City Management Association). These "National Surveys of Employee Benefits for Full-Time Personnel of U.S. Municipalities" were made as of 1970, 1973, and 1976.

Questionnaires were sent out to a large number of cities and towns with populations of at least 10,000 each year (about 1,100 in 1970 and 2,290 in both 1973 and 1976). The numbers of usable questionnaires received were only small proportions of the total sent out (160 in 1970, 581 in 1973, and 777 in 1976). It is likely, therefore, that the replies received are biased toward a greater representation of municipalities having pension plans and, as to indexing provisions for retirement benefits in payment status, possibly biased toward a greater representation of plans with such provisions. It should be recognized that although the response percentages were low, the larger entities tended to submit data relatively more often.[5] Nonetheless, the vast bulk of the number of plans was concentrated among smaller cities and towns. For example, in the 1975 survey, about 40 percent of the plans were in entities with populations of 25,000 to 100,000 and about 50 percent were in even smaller ones.

Questionnaires were also sent out to counties in 1973, but only 16 responses were received, so that data as to pension indexing for this category were not significant.

The 1970 survey inquired as to whether the retirement plan had a provision for automatic postretirement cost-of-living increases. For all plans combined, 35 percent had such a provision (see Table 8). This proportion varied only slightly by type of employee—38 percent for public safety personnel, 34 percent for general employees, and 27 percent for sanitation employees. Somewhat more variation existed by population size of the municipality—43 percent for cities over 100,000, 36 percent for those with 25,000 to 100,000, and 23 percent for those under 25,000 but over 10,000. The trends of the proportion for each employment category varied by population size of the municipality as would be anticipated.

The corresponding proportions in the 1973 and 1975 surveys of municipalities were not greatly different than those in the 1970

---

[5] Certain data from these surveys presented here are not contained in the published reports but have been made available through the kindness of Edward H. Friend & Company, Consulting Actuaries and Employee Benefit Plan Consultants (Washington, D.C.), who conducted the survey project and prepared the reports.

TABLE 8
Data on Automatic-Adjustment Provisions for Pensions in Force under Municipal Retirement Plans

Employment Category	Proportion with Automatics			Proportion of Automatics with Maximum	
	1970	1973	1975	1973	1975
Public safety	38%	33%	34%	63%	71%
Sanitation	27	26	30	71	80
General	34	33	32	78	85
Total	35	32	33	69	77
Size of Municipality					
Over 100,000	43%	34%	36%	70%	73%
25,000–100,000	36	34	34	70	86
10,000–25,000	23	29	31	67	70
Total	35	32	33	69	77

Source: National Surveys of Employee Benefits for Full-Time Personnel of U.S. Municipalities, Labor-Management Relations Service of the National League of Cities, United States Conference of Mayors, and National Association of Counties.

survey. Thus, despite the recent inflationary conditions, there was no discernible trend either to establish automatic-adjustment provisions to alleviate the economic conditions of pensioners, or to eliminate such provisions because of their cost.

The 1973 and 1975 surveys also inquired about whether the automatic-adjustment provisions contained a maximum percentage increase. For plans with automatics, 69 percent did contain a maximum in the 1973 survey, with little variation from this by size of municipality. Significant variation did, however, occur by employment category; only 63 percent of the plans for public safety employees had a maximum, as against 71 percent for sanitation employees and 78 percent for general employees. The 1975 survey showed about the same results, except that there was some indication for all categories of employment and population size of a greater tendency to impose a cap, possibly due to the experience under the inflationary conditions that prevailed after 1973.

CURRENT INDEXING PROVISIONS IN TEACHER RETIREMENT PLANS

Information as to postretirement adjustment of pensions in statewide teacher retirement systems for the 27 states which have such systems is presented in a report of the National Education Association, *Teacher Retirement Systems, A Summary of the 1975 Legal Provisions for Retirement Systems to Which Teachers Belong.* In the other states, teachers are covered by retirement systems including other employees. The report also gives data for 11 large cities which have separate retirement systems for teachers.

Only 9 of the 27 statewide teacher retirement systems have automatic-adjustment provisions. In four plans, the adjustments are routine or guaranteed, independent of CPI changes (one with 1 percent per year, two with 2 percent, and one with 3 percent). Four plans base the increase on the change in the CPI; one sets no maximum on the increase, while the other three have maximums of 1½, 3, and 5 percent respectively. The other plan, New Jersey, bases the increase on half of the rise in the CPI (as described previously as to its plan for general employees). In two plans the increases are effective only after attainment of age 60 or 62.

Only 4 of the 11 city teacher plans have indexing of benefits after retirement. Two plans have routine increases, independent of CPI changes (one at an annual rate of 2 percent after age 60 and the other at 1½ percent after age 71). The other two plans base the increase on changes in the CPI, but with annual maximums (2 percent and 3 percent).

INDEXING PROVISIONS IN STATE AND LOCAL RETIREMENT PLANS ACCORDING TO PENSION TASK FORCE DATA

Perhaps the best current comprehensive source of information about automatic-adjustment provisions for pensions in force among retirement systems for state and local government employees is available from a study made in 1975 by the Pension Task Force of the Committee on Education and Labor of the U.S. House of Representatives.[6] This group made a thorough investigation of all such retirement systems and then conducted a stratified sample study in great depth as to various aspects of such programs. Out of the total of approximately 6,000 such plans, generalized data were available or pertinent for 5,164 plans (the balance being accounted for by either plans incompletely reporting or plans that were inactive or

---

[6] For details of this project and certain preliminary data, see *Interim Report of Activities of the Pension Task Force of the Subcommittee on Labor Standards,* Committee on Education and Labor, U.S. House of Representatives, March 31, 1976.

only for closed groups). The sample included all of the 379 largest plans (at least 1,000 active participants), 200 of the 785 middle-sized plans (at least 100, but less than 1,000 active participants), and 200 of the 4,000 small plans. The results were then appropriately weighted to obtain an estimate for the total universe of such plans.

TABLE 9
Proportion of Retirement Systems for State and Local Government Employees That Have Automatic-Adjustment Provisions for Pensions in Course of Payment, by Size of Plan, 1975

Number of Active Participants in Plan	*Proportion with Automatic-Adjustment Provisions*		*Proportion Where Automatic-Adjustment Provision Has Maximum Limit*	
	By Plans	*By Participants*	*By Plans*	*By Participants*
Adjustment Based on CPI				
Under 100	4.0%	3.0%	80%	70%
100–999	17.0	20.4	90	94
1,000 or more	30.4	34.5	86	89
Total	8.2	33.6	85	89
Adjustment by Constant Percentage				
Under 100	5.6%	10.4%	*	*
100–999	4.5	5.0	*	*
1,000 or more	11.6	16.0	*	*
Total	5.9	15.6	*	*
Adjustment Based on Pay Increases				
Under 100	10.4%	8.7%	*	*
100–999	4.5	4.3	*	*
1,000 or more	3.0	0.7	*	*
Total	8.9	1.0	*	*
Total with Automatic Adjustments				
Under 100	20.0%	22.1%	*	*
100–999	26.0	29.7	*	*
1,000 or more	45.0	51.2	*	*
Total	23.0	50.2	*	*

* Not applicable.
Source of data: Pension Task Force Study, Committee on Education and Labor, U.S. House of Representatives.

Table 9 summarizes the information as to indexing of pensions in course of payment according to size of plan. When considered by number of plans, only 8 percent had automatic-adjustment provisions based on CPI changes, with this proportion being only 4 percent for the smallest plans and increasing to 30 percent for the largest plans. Consequently, when considered by number of participants, the results were quite different, with 34 percent of all participants being in plans with automatic-adjustment features based on the CPI. The only other data on this subject available from the Pension Task Force study was the proportion of plans with such CPI indexing where a maximum limit is imposed on the increases. Such caps were prevalent in the vast majority of the cases, roughly 85 percent. The relatively low proportion with caps for the smallest plans is probably caused by the smallest such plans (i.e., well less than 100 participants) for police and fire employees, because plans for this category are much less likely to have caps than other plans (as will be discussed later.)

A further 6 percent of plans of state and local government employees make automatic adjustments of pensions in course of payment by some constant percentage annually. These provisions tend to be more prevalent in the largest plans. As a result, they are applicable to 16 percent of the participants in such plans.

About 9 percent of these plans have provisions for automatic adjustment of pensions in course of payment according to changes in the general salary level of active employees. As will be discussed later, this procedure is almost entirely confined to plans for police and fire employees, which tend to be small plans, and so it is applicable in plans with only 1 percent of the total participants.

Considering all three types of automatic-adjustment provisions combined, 23 percent of all plans for state and local government employees contain such provisions. However, because such indexing for pensions in course of payment tends to be much more prevalent in the larger plans (and particularly in the very largest ones), the proportion of participants in plans with such provisions is much higher, 50 percent.

Table 10 summarizes further data available from the Pension Task Force study, subdividing the information according to the type of employees covered. Approximately 18 percent of the plans for general employees contain escalation provisions based on the CPI, while these are present in only about 5 percent of the plans for police and fire employees and for teachers. When considered by number of participants, about 40 percent of all general employees are in plans with these indexing features, thus indicating that the largest plans are those that provide such features. Similarly, for the

TABLE 10
Proportion of Retirement Systems for State and Local Government Employees That Have Automatic-Adjustment Provisions for Pensions in Course of Payment, by Type of Employee Covered, 1975

Type of Employee Covered	Proportion with Automatic-Adjustment Provisions		Proportion Where Automatic-Adjustment Provision Has Maximum Limit	
	By Plans	By Participants	By Plans	By Participants
Adjustment Based on CPI				
Police and fire	4.9%	18.0%	73%	68%
Teachers	4.1	23.4	85	89
General†	17.8	39.7	93	89
Total...........	8.2	33.6	85	89
Adjustment by Constant Percentage				
Police and fire	6.3%	6.9%	*	*
Teachers	2.3	21.9	*	*
General†	5.8	13.1	*	*
Total...........	5.9	15.6	*	*
Adjustment Based on Pay Increase				
Police and fire	12.2%	11.2%	*	*
Teachers	—	—	*	*
General†	3.2	0.7	*	*
Total...........	8.9	1.0	*	*
Total with Automatic Adjustments				
Police and fire	23.4%	36.1%	*	*
Teachers	6.4	45.3	*	*
General†	26.8	53.5	*	*
Total...........	23.0	50.2	*	*

* Not applicable.
† Includes plans covering both general employees and police and fire personnel and/or teachers.
Source of data: Pension Task Force Study, Committee on Education and Labor, U.S. House of Representatives.

teachers and the police and fire employees, there is clear evidence that the larger plans contain indexing provisions. For plans that have these automatic-adjustment provisions, about 90 percent of those for teachers and for general employees contain a cap on the amount of the early increase, but for police and fire employees, provision of a cap is much less frequent (in only about 70 percent of the cases).

An additional 6 percent of the pension plans for police and fire employees contain provisions for automatic-adjustment of pensions in course of payment by a uniform percentage each year.

Such proportion is 2 percent for plans for teachers and 6 percent for plans for general employees. Such a type of provision is more prevalent in the larger plans, as noted previously, and so the proportions of participants in such plans are higher than the proportions of plans.

Virtually none of the plans for teachers and for general employees adjust pensions according to changes in the salary level for active employees. This procedure, however, is used in 12 percent of such plans for police and fire employees, and here there seems to be about the same usage of this basis among both small and large plans.

About 23 percent of the plans for state and local government employees, with 50 percent of the participants, contain one of the three types of automatic-adjustment provisions. For plans for teachers, such provisions were present in 6 percent of the plans (with 45 percent of the participants). On the other hand, this proportion was only 23 percent by plans (and 36 percent by participants) in plans for police and fire employees, and 27 percent by plans (but as high as 54 percent by participants) in plans for general employees.

GENERAL CONCLUSIONS AS TO INDEXING PROVISIONS IN STATE AND LOCAL RETIREMENT PLANS

In summary, automatic adjustment of pensions after retirement is quite common among systems for state and local government employees but is by no means universal. Such indexing occurs in slightly more than half of the statewide retirement systems for general employees (in some cases, other employees such as teachers are also included). In statewide plans covering teachers exclusively, somewhat less than half contain indexing provisions. Only about one third of city and town retirement systems provide automatic adjustments. In general, such provisions are most likely to be found in the larger states and cities.

Most retirement systems of state and local governments that provide indexing of pensions do so on the basis of changes in the CPI, although generally with a cap on the annual increase (which, in recent years, has always been applicable in the actual operation of the provision); under such circumstances, however, almost universally any CPI increase not utilized is carried over to subsequent years.[7] The remainder have a routine or guaranteed increase that occurs regardless of the change in the CPI, but in such an amount that, at least in recent years, it is well below the CPI rise. Some plans contain other limitations—for example, the indexing is not applicable during the first few years of retirement or until a certain age has been attained. When the CPI is used for adjustment purposes, almost always the CPI for all items for the United States as a whole is utilized, but in a few instances the CPI for the locality is adopted.[8]

---

[7] For example, if the annual maximum is 3 percent, and the CPI rises by 4 percent, then the excess 1 percent is available in later years when the CPI increases less than 3 percent. Thus, if in the next year the CPI rise was only 1½ percent, the pensions would be increased by 2½ percent.

[8] For example, the retirement system for Montgomery County, Md. (near Washington, D.C.) uses the CPI for the Metropolitan Washington area.

Indexing of Governmental Benefits in Canada

Canada provides an even greater extent of indexing in various governmental benefit programs than does the United States. These provisions generally became effective in the past decade, following the enactment of the Canada Pension Plan in 1965. In the early 1970s, this approach was extended so that it now applies to almost all social benefit programs. At the same time, indexing of pensions in force has been widely adopted in the retirement systems for federal and provincial employees.

This chapter will first deal with the indexing provisions in the national pension program of Canada and will then describe how indexing applies in other federal social benefit programs. Finally, the automatic-adjustment provisions in the pension plans for federal and provincial employees will be discussed.

INDEXING OF FEDERAL SOCIAL BENEFITS PROGRAMS

Old-Age Security Benefits

Before the enactment of the Canada Pension Plan (to be discussed hereafter), Canada provided flat-rate benefits on a demogrant basis, with qualification solely by reason of residence and age (initially age 70, but beginning in 1966, gradually phased down until reaching age 65 in 1970). These payments (termed Old-Age Security) are financed out of general revenues, although some years ago they were approximately financed by certain earmarked general taxes.

The OAS payments in January 1952 were at the rate of $40 per month, and increased on an ad hoc basis several times until reaching $75 in October 1963. The 1965 legislation provided for indexing, beginning in 1968, on the basis of the Pension Index. This index for any particular year was originally defined as the average of the monthly CPIs for the 12 months ending with the previous June, except that the index could never exceed 102 percent of the preceding year's index. Further, if the index did not raise by at least 1 percent, no change in the benefits would be made, but then any such unused increases would be available for future possible increases. Under the inflationary conditions prevailing in the late 1960s and early 1970s, the Pension Index rose by the full 2 percent each year, increasing from 109.3 for 1967 to 123.1 for 1973.

However, in 1971 the indexing principle was abandoned for OAS and the monthly payment was frozen at $80 (as compared to $79.58 for 1970). For 1972, however, indexing was reintroduced, but without the 2 percent annual limit. The first increase was 3.6 percent. The annual adjustments were to be made each April on the basis of the full CPI change, as measured by a 12-month average with a 6-month lag.

Then, with the continuing high inflation, an ad hoc increase in the OAS benefit to $100 was made for April 1973, and again to $105.30 for October 1973. Commencing thereafter indexing has been applied quarterly, instead of annually. Such quarterly indexing is no longer done by the Pension Index (which is used, after modification, in the Canada Pension Plan). Rather, for benefits for a particular quarter, comparison of the average CPI for the third, fourth, and fifth months preceding such quarter is made with that for the sixth, seventh, and eighth preceding months. The resulting percentage increase is then applied to the previous benefit rate, after rounding such increase to the nearest 0.1 percent and not permitting a decrease (under such circumstances, the base quarter before the decrease remains applicable for subsequent quarters until there is an increase).

Canada Pension Plan Benefits

The Canada Pension Plan is a contributory social insurance system providing earnings-related benefits. It was enacted in 1965 and went into operation in 1966, with benefits first being payable the next year (but at relatively low rates because they are proportional to length of coverage for the first ten years). At the same time, a separate Quebec Pension Plan went into operation in that province, with provisions which have, over the years, closely approximated those of the CPP. In the subsequent discussion it should be understood that unless otherwise stated, the QPP has the same provisions as the CPP.[1]

The CPP provided not only for indexing of benefits in course of payment but also for indexing of the maximum earnings subject to taxation and credit for benefits and of the past earnings record (when benefit amounts are computed). The earnings base was to be adjusted according to the Pension Index during 1968–75 (which, as indicated previously, involved a 2 percent maximum annual increase), and thereafter on the basis of a national earnings index. In practice, such adjustment of the earnings base was made until 1973, but beginning with 1974, ad hoc, larger increases were provided. Currently, the law provides that the earnings base shall be increased by 12½ percent each year until it reaches approximately the average earnings of all workers in the country, and thereafter it is to be maintained at that standard.

In computing CPP benefits, the past actual earnings record in terms of dollars is indexed (or revalued). This is done by multiplying the actual credited earnings for a given year by the ratio of the average of the maximum earnings base for the three years ending with the year when the pension becomes payable to the earnings base for the given year.

CPP benefits in course of payment are automatically adjusted by the Pension Index referred to previously. Specifically, the benefit amount for a particular year is obtained by multiplying the benefit amount for the previous year by the increase in the Pension Index applicable to the particular year. The only exception to this indexing is with regard to children of disabled and deceased workers under the QPP, for whom no automatic adjustment of benefits is made.

---

[1] For more details on the CPP as it was initially constituted, see Daniel S. Gehrig and Robert J. Myers, "Canada Pension Plan of 1965," *Social Security Bulletin*, November 1965.

As indicated previously, the Pension Index was subject to a maximum annual increase of 2 percent prior to 1973. In that year the 2 percent cap continued for the CPP, but was increased to 3 percent for the QPP. Then in 1974, under both the CPP and the QPP, the cap was completely removed.[2] At the same time, the measurement of the change in the CPI was made with a shorter lag than the six-month one prevailing previously. Specifically, the Pension Index for a particular year is now the average of the CPI during the 12-month period ending with the previous October.[3] As before, the Pension Index is rounded to the nearest 0.1 percent, and no decrease in it is recognized for purposes of computing benefit amounts.

Other Federal Social Benefits

Canada has an income-tested program that supplements OAS, designated as Guaranteed Income Supplement. Also, the spouse's allowance under OAS (which is an income-tested payment for spouses aged 60 and over) is indexed in the same manner as OAS benefits. The benefit levels of these two programs are automatically adjusted in the same way as is OAS.

The Family Allowance program, which makes payments to all children under age 18 (flat amounts, differing somewhat by province, financed largely by the federal government through a uniform monthly average payment per child, which the province can redistribute by varying payment sizes by age of child or family size). These benefits are subject to indexing annually, on the basis of changes in the CPI in the same manner as the CPP, with the federal payment per child being so adjusted. Such indexing was suspended in 1976, but it has subsequently been restored.

The Unemployment Insurance program also is indexed insofar as the maximum taxable earnings base and the maximum weekly benefit are concerned. The indexing is done annually, on the basis of changes in average earnings for the country as a whole (as determined from census survey data).

Veterans pensions are automatically adjusted, using the same procedure as the CPP.

---

[2] When this was done, the pensions in force were adjusted upward to reflect the increases in the CPI in the past that had not been recognized because of the cap.

[3] For the changeover year (1974), the applicable Pension Index was the average of the CPI in the 16-month period ending October 1973.

Although the income tax is hardly a social benefit, it is interesting to note that certain of its provisions are automatically adjusted to reflect changes in economic conditions. The major personal exemptions and standard deductions and the dollar brands in the tax brackets are determined by indexing based on the CPI. The adjustment factor for any particular year, which is applied to the values for the preceding year, is the ratio of the CPI for the 12-month period ending the previous September to the CPI for the preceding 12-month period. The adjustments first became operative for 1974. The resulting figures for personal exemptions and standard deductions are rounded so as to be an even $10, while those for the tax brackets are rounded to the nearest dollar. Once again, decreases are not provided for in the event that the CPI goes down.

WORKERS' COMPENSATION PROGRAMS

The workers' compensation system (for work-connected accidents and diseases) in Canada is based on separate programs in each of the provinces.[4] Indexing provisions are present in some of these programs with respect to two elements.

In several provinces, the maximum periodic benefit is determined from 75 percent of an earnings base that is varied annually according to changes in average wages in the jurisdiction (as is done in a number of state programs in the United States). Several other provinces have a unique approach in this respect. In Manitoba and Saskatchewan, the earnings base is increased by $1,000 if 10 percent of the new beneficiaries had an earnings rate in excess of the base, while Newfoundland follows a somewhat similar procedure.

Periodic benefits in course of payment are indexed for changes in the CPI in several provinces (semiannually in British Columbia and annually in Nova Scotia and Quebec). Although in previous years there were maximums imposed on these increases (such as 2 percent per year), now no limitations are involved.

INDEXING OF PENSIONS FOR GOVERNMENTAL EMPLOYEES

Beginning in 1968, the pensions paid to retired federal employees and their survivors have been escalated automatically on the basis

---

[4] For a summary of the provisions of these programs, see *Analysis of Workers' Compensation Laws, 1978 Edition,* (Washington, D.C.: Chamber of Commerce of the United States January 1, 1978).

of changes in the CPI. Initially, there was a maximum of 2 percent on the annual increase (with any unused amount being carried forward for years when the increase is more than 2 percent). In the actual experience, the 2 percent maximum was always applicable, until in 1973 the limit was eliminated.

The adjustment in this federal civil service plan is now made annually (for calendar years) in the same manner and on the same general basis as under the CPP (i.e., with decreases not being possible and with the percentage change being based on the CPI in base years ending with September—rather than October as in the CPP—and being rounded to the nearest 0.1 percent). The automatic adjustment is applicable to all pensioners on the roll for December, regardless of whether they had just retired or whether they had been on the roll for years, thus creating an anomalous situation as between those who retire just after the close of the year as against those retiring just before then. Such indexing is also applicable during the deferred period for those separating from service with vested pensions (when these become payable). It may be noted that the minimum retirement ages for general employees are 55 with 30 years of service and 60 with 5–29 years of service.

The pension plans for the armed forces and for the Royal Canadian Mounted Police are indexed in the same manner as that for federal civilian employees. Indexing is applicable immediately for disability pensioners (or at later onset of disability for age pensioners not otherwise receiving indexing). For age pensioners, indexing is done at age 60 in any case or at ages 55–59 when the sum of the attained age and the years of service equals at least 85 (i.e., in all cases of retirement at ages 55–59 with at least 30 years of service—as well as other cases where the total of age and service is at least 85). Survivor pensions are indexed immediately after entry on the roll. When indexing is started at some time after initial entry on the roll (e.g., for an age pensioner at age 60 when age and service total less then 85), it is based on the year of retirement up to the current time.

A restriction on the indexing was temporarily introduced for 1976 (when there were national wage controls). Then, a limit of $2,400 on the annual pension amount was imposed on the increase that occurred from the 11.3 percent rise generally applicable; this paralleled the ceiling imposed on wage increases. This, however, affected less than 200 persons on the rolls of the federal government employee pension plans.

Under all the pension plans for federal employees, a separate fund is created to pay out the benefit escalations. These funds are financed by a contribution rate of 1 percent from the member and a like amount from the government (until recently, ½ percent each), except that the federal government, beginning in 1974, pays the entire cost for indexing the benefits of those who retired before 1970. The employee contributions are refundable (with interest) upon separation from service without vested pension rights. There is, of course, no certainty that the financing currently provided is sufficient over the long range (although it could be more than sufficient if inflation should diminish).

Recently, much public concern had been expressed about the liberal indexing provisions in these pension plans for government employees, especially as compared with those of pension plans for private employees. As a result, the federal government studied the matter and, in early 1978, made certain proposals for change.[5] One change would provide only prorata adjustments for new retirees who had been on the roll less than one year at the effective date of the pension increase, rather than the full annual increase. A second change would eliminate any indexing before age 60 for age pensioners (but not for disability or survivor pensioners); at age 60, however, the full increase from time of retirement to age 60 would be given for future pension payments.[6] This change would be phased in over a 5–year period. Third, and perhaps most importantly, the indexing would be limited, over 3–year future periods, by what it would be estimated could be financed by the available resources. Such resources are: (1) the combined employer-employee contributions allocated for this purpose (1 percent each); (2) the accumulated fund from such contributions in the past; and (3) the "excess interest" earnings of the portion of the fund allocated to pensioners (i.e., based on the excess of the actual investment rate of return—currently, about 7½ percent— over a real interest rate, such as 3½ or 4 percent). If the resources appear to be insufficient to support full escalation, the indexing

---

[5] Under the Canadian legislative procedure, a formal proposal by the executive branch is virtually tantamount to eventual enactment, because the executive branch is always headed by the leader of the majority party in the Parliament, and members of Parliament are under strict party discipline.

[6] For example, if a person retired in January at age 55, and if the CPI increased by 30 percent over the next five years, the pension amount would remain level over that period, but would then be increased by 30 percent at age 60 (and such higher pension would then be automatically adjusted in the future).

would be scaled down (e.g., equally proportionate for all pensions or full indexing for small pensions and lower indexing for higher pension amounts).

Some of the pension plans for employees of the several provincial governments have utilized only ad hoc procedures to increase pensions for changes in economic conditions. In others, however, indexing provisions are applicable, following the lead of the federal government. These can be summarized in the following manner as of mid-1978:

1. *British Columbia.* Adjustments in January and July, based on changes in the CPI, no maximum (first adjustment in the January or July that occurs more than six months after the month of retirement).
2. *New Brunswick.* Annual adjustments based on changes in the CPI, 6 percent maximum; additional employee contribution rate of ½ percent for this provision.
3. *Nova Scotia.* Annual adjustments based on changes in the CPI, 4 percent maximum generally, but higher maximums for lower pensions.
4. *Ontario.* Annual adjustments based on changes in the CPI, 8 percent maximum; additional employee contribution rate of 1 percent for this provision.[7]
5. *Prince Edward Island.* Annual adjustments based on changes in the CPI, 8 percent maximum.
6. *Quebec.* Annual adjustment based on changes in the CPI, no maximum.

In several instances, these provincial plans have been liberalized in recent years as inflation rose. For example, a few years ago, Nova Scotia had a 2 percent cap, and New Brunswick had an automatic 2 percent increase regardless of changes in economic conditions.

Unlike the situation in the United States, no Canadian retirement systems for governmental employees have automatic adjustment of pensions in force by guaranteed percentage increases regardless of CPI changes or by increases based on changes in the salary level of active employees.

---

[7] Despite the liberal indexing provision for employees of this province, it is interesting to note that the unified retirement system for the more than 100,000 employees in almost 1,000 municipalities of this province does not contain any such provision. It does, however, increase pensions in course of payment by any favorable investment results.

Indexing of Pensions in Foreign Social Security Programs*

This chapter will present an overview of the provisions that are made in social security programs of countries outside of North America to index pension payments for changes in economic conditions. Naturally, with such a great diversity of programs and approaches, complete treatment of this subject is not possible. Before taking up the subject of indexing of pensions in course of payment, several related subjects will be considered.

GENERAL INDEXING PROCEDURES

Many countries in the period following World War II had much greater inflationary pressures (or expected to have them) than did the United States. As a result, more attention was devoted to indexing various economic components of the society, including social

---

* The discussion in this chapter is based largely on material published in several papers and notes in the *Social Security Bulletin* (March 1960, May 1970, July 1974, April 1976, and November 1976); in the various biennial issues of *Social Security Programs throughout the World,* Social Security Administration; in various issues of the *International Social Security Review,* International Social Security Association; in various issues of *IBIS* (*International Benefits Information Service*), Charles D. Spencer & Associates, Inc., Chicago; and in *Pensions and Inflation,* International Labor Office, 1977.

security programs. One such component, of course, was the general level of wages. Another was the instruments of financial indebtedness (bonds, mortgages, loans, etc.), which are of significance in the financing of both social insurance systems and private pension plans.

Index-linked bonds and other similar types of indebtedness are those under which both the interest payments and the principal amount due at maturity are adjusted according to some economic index. This, of course, can be extremely valuable in the funding of a pension plan with indexation of benefits. This approach was adopted in Finland shortly after World War II and became widely used in both the public and private sectors in the next two decades. However, in 1967, this procedure (as well as that applicable to wages) was terminated due to fear that it would worsen inflationary trends.

On the other hand, Israel adopted index-linked bonds in 1948 and has continued to do so ever since.[1] Although Israel has had considerable continuing inflation, apparently the indexing procedure has been thought workable. Beginning in 1967, Brazil has had quite complete indexing in its economic operations. Once again, although inflation has continued (but at somewhat lower rates than the very high rates previously), it seems to be thought by some that the indexing has been helpful, although some economists have been critical of this procedure.

INDEXING PROCEDURES PRIOR TO RETIREMENT

Many countries recognize changes in economic conditions during the work careers of employees by either using a final type of average salary or indexing the entire earnings record. Such indexing was first adopted by the Federal Republic of Germany (West), France, and Sweden in the late 1950s. Since then, a number of other countries have this approach (Algeria, Austria, Belgium, Canada, Chile, Norway, Portugal, Switzerland, Turkey, and Yugoslavia). The indexing is done on the basis of wage, salary, or

---

[1] Strangely, in the author's view, the index-linked government bonds issued to the social security system bear a relatively high interest rate (6 percent). One would reasonably suppose that if both interest payments and principal are adjusted for changes in prices or purchasing power, the applicable interest rate would be at about the "real" or inherent rate of 3 percent.

earnings trends or, in some instances, price trends.[2] In practice, several countries which index by prices have made ad hoc changes from time to time that had the effect of producing total increases about equal to what indexing by wages would have brought about; this was done because of the inadequacies and inconsistencies that are produced when earnings records are indexed only for price changes.

It may be noted that the decoupling proposals recommended by the Advisory Council on Social Security in 1975, supported by the Ford and Carter Administrations, and enacted into law in December 1977, were based on indexing of the earnings record by wage trends (see Chapter 4).

INDEXING PROCEDURES AFTER RETIREMENT

In the post–World War II period, many countries have found it necessary to increase social security benefit levels to offset the effects of inflation. In some nations, as in the United States, reliance initially was placed on ad hoc methods by which the legislatures or the responsible authorities increased the benefit level by arbitrary amounts (often approximating the changes in the cost of living or price level). Later, semiautomatic or automatic procedures were adopted, so as to have more specific guidelines for action.

Under semiautomatic procedures, the amount of the increase is determined mathematically, according to prescribed conditions, but it does not become effective until approved by the responsible authorities (such as the legislature or a special council established for this particular purpose). If such approval is not given, the responsible authorities may institute a different increase. In any

---

[2] France and Germany index on the basis of wages, while Belgium and Sweden index on the basis of prices, and Norway does so on a mixed earnings-prices basis. The Swedish procedure is accomplished indirectly—by converting actual credited wages into "pension points," which relate the actual wages to a "base amount" that, in turn, is adjusted automatically for changes in prices (the mathematical effect is exactly the same as if the earnings record itself were indexed by prices). For more details on this subject, see Chapters 1–3 of *Protecting Social Security Beneficiary Earnings against Inflation: The Foreign Experience*, Staff Paper No. 25 (Washington, D.C.: Office of Research and Statistics, Social Security Administration, September 1976). This paper also applies the techniques used in six foreign countries to the earnings of what is termed "a typical American worker retiring at age 65 in 1970" to show what the result would have been; the author of this monograph does not believe that the results are meaningful because of insufficient long-term data and because the case is not really "typical," the wage increasing only 9.0 percent from 1960 to 1970, as against the general trend of wages showing an increase of 51 percent.

event, the action is taken by promulgation or, at times, by specific new legislation.

Automatic procedures, as the name implies, occur entirely by action of the administering authorities, who follow the prescribed methodology as to computation and timing as contained in the pertinent law or regulation. In practice, it is difficult (or even impossible) under some circumstances to distinguish between the semiautomatic and automatic bases. For example, in the U.S. OASDI system, it could be said that the procedure is not really automatic because the law prescribes that it is to be suspended if Congress takes ad hoc action.

Then, too, considering political and social pressures, it is not often that the semiautomatic procedure will result in significant changes from what a completely automatic procedure would have done because the reviewing body will not usually act to change the indicated action. In the discussion hereafter, no distinction will be made as between semiautomatic and automatic adjustment methods.

The trend in recent years has been to make the adjustments more on a current basis so that the benefit increase occurs more promptly after the economic change that caused it. At times when sharp spurts of inflation have occurred, there have been some actions to spread the resulting determined benefit increase over a longer period in order to have a smoothing-out effect.

In this respect, it is important to note that even though inflation is at a high level, the length of lag involved between the measuring period and the effective date of the benefit change has no permanent effect *if the rate of inflation remains constant.* When the rate increases sharply at any one time, the benefit adjustment is tardy, and the beneficiaries suffer reduced purchasing power during the lag period (and even beyond for a time). However, when the reverse occurs later, the beneficiaries will catch up, and the increase will cause the purchasing power of their benefits to rise and come back toward where it originally was (or possibly even go higher).

Denmark was the first nation to adopt indexing procedures for pensions in course of payment. Such provisions, based on changes in the cost of living, were introduced in 1922, but they were repealed in 1927 and then reenacted in 1933.

The next countries to adopt indexing procedures were Iceland and Luxembourg, in 1948. However, as a result of roaring inflation,

Iceland eliminated the automatic-adjustment provisions in the late 1960s (although making ad hoc adjustments thereafter). Next, came France in 1948, using a unique method of indexing by earnings. The data used are the average daily cash benefits paid under the national temporary disability program. Such cash benefits, in turn, are based on the average covered earnings of insured workers.

Sweden, in 1950, adopted indexing of pensions in course of payment for its program of flat-rate benefits. When an earnings-related system supplementary to the flat-rate one was enacted in 1959, the same indexing procedure was made applicable. In both instances, adjustment is made according to changes in the CPI, with a 3 percent trigger (originally 5 percent), and downward movements are permitted. At times in the past, additional ad hoc increases have been given, so as to provide beneficiaries with some share of the national rise in productivity (i.e., wages having increased more rapidly than prices).

Chile was the first American nation to institute indexing of pensions in force, in 1952. However, because of catastrophic inflation, it was compelled to suspend these procedures in 1957; they were later reinstituted, but based on price changes, rather than wage changes, as initially.

When Israel inaugurated its flat-rate pension program in 1953, it included automatic-adjustment provisions based on price changes. In 1974, the adjustment procedure was changed so as to be based on wage changes.

In 1956, both West Germany and the Netherlands adopted indexing for pensions in course of payment. In West Germany, which has earnings-related benefits, the adjustment is on the basis of earnings changes, with about a three-year lag involved as between the date of measurement of the change and the date when benefits are increased. As discussed previously, over the long run, this lag does not have any significant effect on the relative maintenance of the purchasing power of the benefits over the period of their receipt.[3] The flat-rate benefits of the Netherlands are adjusted on the basis of a wage index, with a 3 percent trigger and semiannual adjustments.

As of 1960, nine countries, mostly European, had adopted indexing for pensions in course of payment. In the 1960s, eight more

[3] It should be noted, however, that the *initial* level is reduced by the lag being long, because the pension is a certain percentage of an indexed average earnings where the lag in indexing means a lower base. Accordingly, the postretirement indexing, on the average, maintains the relative value of the somewhat reduced initial pension.

countries took such action, while Iceland eliminated its automatic escalation. As of 1970, there were thus 16 countries (11 of them in Europe) having automatic-adjustment provisions, while by 1975 this number had increased to 33 (only 16 of them in Europe). Table 11 shows the specific nations involved and the methods utilized.

TABLE 11
Countries with Provisions for Automatic Adjustment of National Pensions in Force, by Basis of Indexing

Indexing by Prices	Indexing by Wages	Indexing by Minimum Wage	Indexing by Mixture of Prices and Wages
	Procedure Adopted before 1960		
Belgium	Israel*		
Chile†	Netherlands		
Denmark			
Finland (flat)			
Iceland‡			
Luxembourg			
Sweden			
	Procedure Adopted in 1960–69		
Canada	Argentina		Norway
Italy¶	Austria		
	Finland (wage related)		
	France		
	Germany (West)		
	Uruguay		
	Procedure Adopted in 1970–75		
Colombia	Bolivia	Brazil	
Ecuador	Spain	Malagasy	
El Salvador	United Kingdom (flat)	Mexico	
Japan			
New Zealand			
Portugal			
Switzerland§			
United Kingdom (wage related)‖			
United States			
Upper Volta			
Yugoslavia			
Zaire			

* Initially indexing was on the basis of changes in prices (see text).

† Initially indexing was on the basis of changes in wages (see text).

‡ Indexing ceased in the late 1960s.

§ In 1977, changed to an index combining prices and wages.

‖ For United Kingdom, as of current (1977) law. For flat-benefit system, indexing is done by prices when this is more favorable to the beneficiaries (which will not often be the case).

¶ In 1976, changed to a basis such that minimum pensions are adjusted by changes in wages (if this is more than the adjustment by prices); for pensions above the minimum, one portion is adjusted for wage changes, and the remainder is adjusted for price changes.

The three countries which make the adjustment according to changes in the nationally prescribed minimum wage are difficult to classify because in some instances this element is basically determined from changes in prices.

It is interesting to note that Finland and the United Kingdom have both flat-rate and earnings-related benefit systems and that currently they use different indexes for each. In Finland, the flat-rate benefits are adjusted by price changes, while the earnings-related benefits are adjusted by wage changes. On the other hand, in the United Kingdom, essentially the reverse situation prevails.

The development of indexing in the United Kingdom is worthy of somewhat more detailed consideration. Beginning in 1971, annual reviews were provided for as to the situation under the flat-benefit program, considering both changes in prices and wages. The resulting adjustments were made essentially on whichever of these two elements increased more rapidly (i.e., wages generally). In addition, at times after 1971, ad hoc increases were made. The benefits under the new earnings-related program, which goes into effect in 1978, will be adjusted according to changes in the cost of living after the beneficiary has gone onto the rolls.

Almost universally, indexing of pensions in force is done on a "historical" basis. The actual experience as to the relevant economic factor for some past period is applied to the benefits payable beginning at some time in the future after the date of determination and promulgation. There is thus a double lag—from the end of the last experience period to the date of determination and from the latter date to the effective date of the benefit change.

The United Kingdom program, beginning in 1976, obviates this disadvantage of having lags by using a "forecast" method. Under this procedure, the adjustments are made on the basis of estimates of what the situation will be on the effective date of the last previous change. For example, in the review made in May 1976, the rate of increase to be first applicable to benefits for November 1976 was determined from the actual data for November 1975 and the estimated forecast for November 1976.[4] Then, if the actual data for

---

[4] The previous review, made in May 1975, used the "historical" procedure, basing the benefit change on the increase in earnings levels (which was larger than the increase in prices) in the seven-month period ending March 1975. The change was measured over seven months because this was the period from the date of the last previous benefit increase (an ad hoc one), April 1975, to the intended effective date of the new increase, November 1975. If the "historical" method had been used to determine the increase for November 1976, the

November 1976 differs from the forecast, an appropriate adjustment would be made at the time of the next review.

In 1977, Switzerland revised its method of automatically adjusting pensions in course of payment by shifting from an index based
on prices alone to one based on the average of a price index and a
wage index. Adjustments are to be made on a biennial basis, but
this may be accelerated if the price index increases more than 8
percent in a single year and may be postponed if such index rises
less than 5 percent in two years.

The social insurance systems of the Iron Curtain countries, with
the exception of the Hungarian one, do not contain automatic-
adjustment provisions for pensions in course of payment but rather
use ad hoc methods. In Hungary, however, there is a routine,
guaranteed increase of 2 percent per year (with a minimum increase in monetary terms for small pensions). This is intended to
compensate for the planned likely increase in the price level due to
purchases from the capitalist nations. In addition, ad hoc benefit
increases are made whenever centrally planned price rises of basic
consumer goods or services are made as being "unavoidable," so
as to compensate pensioners for the impact of such measures.

West Germany, despite its generally strong economic position,
felt compelled in 1978 to suspend its automatic-adjustment provisions for pensions in course of payment. Instead of escalating
by changes in wages, the 1979–81 increases will be ad hoc ones—
4.5 percent in 1979 and 4.0 percent in both 1980 and 1981. Such
increases are expected to be in excess of price rises, but below
wage rises. After 1981, the automatics will take over again.

---

measurement period would have been March 1975 to March 1976, and this would have
resulted in a considerably larger increase than actually occurred under the "projection"
procedure (because of the very high rate of inflation in March–October 1975, as compared
with what was projected for April–November 1976—the period November 1975 to March
1976 being common to both procedures).

Indexing of Benefits of
Private Pension Plans

The indexing of pension benefits after retirement in private pension plans is much less common than in social security programs or pension plans for government employees. Inflationary conditions and their effect on pensions in course of payment have been widely recognized by ad hoc increases under private pension plans, often based on changes in a consumer price index.

Probably, the major reason for not having automatic-adjustment provisions in private pension plans is the element of fiscal caution against becoming involved in provisions that can involve unpredictable, very high—or, under some circumstances, even catastrophic—costs. It may, however, be said on the other side of the question that much of such cost does arise anyhow in practice through ad hoc adjustments and that the financing required would not seem too onerous if the valuation interest rate used were set at the realistic level of about 3 percent, and the excess interest earnings obtained were used for this purpose (as was discussed in Chapter 2).

Disability pensions are often provided outside of pension plans, through group long-term disability insurance (LTD). Most LTD plans provide level payments once the individual has started receiving benefits, but in a few plans automatic adjustment is made for changes in the CPI, generally with a cap of 2 or 3 percent a year (and a floor of the initial amount).[1]

Defined-benefit plans (which can make adjustment for inflation before retirement in a rational way by using a final-average-wage procedure) can index pensions in course of payment if the sponsor is willing to bear the additional cost. However, strictly speaking, a defined contribution (money-purchase) plan cannot have automatic adjustments for CPI changes after retirement. Although, both before and after retirement, investment performance could provide the financing needed for adjustment for inflation, there is no assurance that it would suffice. Many defined-contribution plans do provide for distribution of "excess" interest (i.e., the excess of the rate actually earned over the guaranteed rate), both in the accumulation period before retirement and to pensions in course of payment.

Of course, the sponsor of a defined-contribution plan could provide the additional funds for postretirement indexing, but then some would say that the plan no longer was a pure defined-contribution one. Within the framework of a defined-contribution plan, however, routine or guaranteed automatic annual increases could be provided on an actuarial-equivalent basis, and these would go at least part way toward maintaining the purchasing power of the pensions in times of inflationary conditions.

This chapter will discuss the various ways in which pensions in course of payment under private plans are automatically adjusted and the extent of such provisions. Separate treatment will be given for the situation in the United States as against that in Canada and in other foreign countries. The analysis, however, cannot be made in the same depth as it was for social security programs or pension plans for government employees because survey and other data are not as readily available.

---

[1] The initial amount is generally determined by offsetting any social security benefit payable (in some cases only the primary benefit, and in other cases the total family benefit) or any other governmental benefit payable (such as from a state workers' compensation or temporary disability insurance plan) from the LTD "formula amount." Some years ago, any increases in the social security benefit arising after entry on the roll were also offset against the LTD benefit, but this is rarely done currently (partly because of being prohibited in some states and partly because of the apparently illogical results and the consequent complaints of the beneficiaries). One large life insurance company that was one of the first to offer such a provision (in 1969) currently has only five plans with such a provision out of a total of about 550 LTD plans.

INDEXING IN PRIVATE PENSION PLANS IN THE UNITED STATES

Although the benefits payable to retirees under the social security program in the United States and those under virtually all retirement systems for federal civilian and military employees are indexed (as well as a large proportion of the retirement systems for state and local government employees), this is by no means the case in pension plans for employees in private industry. Perhaps for this reason, relatively little summary information has been collected on indexing of private pensions.

Probably the first private pension plan in the United States to adopt automatic escalation of benefits after retirement was that of National Airlines.[2] This provision was developed in 1954. The technical work involved was performed jointly by Geoffrey N. Calvert, a consulting actuary, and G. Warfield Hobbs, vice president, First National City Bank, both of whom had been working independently in this general field and who were requested to develop a specific plan by G. T. Baker, president of National Airlines. Mr. Baker had a uniquely personal interest in this area because his father had been with a company that established a pension plan in 1914 with a benefit level of $100 per month, which at that time seemed quite adequate. Later, however, when his father retired, the purchasing power of the pension had declined significantly.

Currently, National Airlines has several different pension plans for various categories of employees. The plans for pilots and for communications employees compute the initial pension amount under the career-average approach, but with each unit of pension for a particular year of service being adjusted by the change in the CPI from the time of accrual to the time of retirement. Such percentage adjustment of the earnings record for a particular year, however, cannot exceed 7½ percent times the number of years from such year to the time of retirement.

It is interesting to note that this approach bears a great similarity to the recommendations of the Consultant Panel to the Congressional Research Service with regard to decoupling of the social security program through a CPI indexing method, as described in

---

[2] The following papers may be of interest with regard to this plan: Geoffrey N. Calvert, "Cost-of-Living Pension Plan," *Harvard Business Review,* September–October 1954; and Alexander G. Hardy, "National Airlines' Cost-of-Living Plan," in *Controlling Employee Benefit and Pension Costs,* Special Report No. 23 (New York: American Management Association, 1975).

Chapter 4. It is also interesting to note that this procedure under the National Airlines plan generally gives a relatively lower initial pension than would a final-average approach (assuming the same percentage factors per year of service)—in somewhat the same way as the Average Indexed Monthly Earnings under the decoupling procedures which had been proposed for the social security program differed as between CPI indexing and wage indexing.

The National Airlines plans for the following categories also indexed the earnings record in this manner at times in the past, but they have ceased doing so (after the month indicated): flight engineers (December 1962); flight superintendents (July 1967); mechanical, stores, and related employees (December 1968); and clerical, office, and station employees (April 1970). When the change was made, the career-average basis was continued, but the benefit percentage factors were significantly increased.

Under the National Airlines plan for pilots and communications employees, every six months after retirement the pension amounts are varied according to changes in the CPI. Specifically, the average CPI for the 24-month period measured back from the second month before the month of retirement is used as the base, and such average CPI for the second month before the month when the pension amount is to be adjusted is compared with it. A lag in the pension change is provided. The first 5 percent increase in the CPI is disregarded, and the pension amount is increased only for CPI rises above 5 percent. Similarly, if the CPI decreases, no adjustment is made below the original amount until there has been at least a 10 percent drop below it, and then only decreases in excess thereof are considered.

Thus, the original amount of the pension remains unchanged if the CPI stays within the range of 5 percent above and 10 percent below its value when the person retired (or the amount reverts to the original value if the CPI has gone outside of this range and then reverts to it). Specifically, if the CPI rises by 8 percent from the time the individual retires, the pension is increased 3 percent; then, if the CPI drops to 4 percent above the initial base, the pension is reduced to the original amount, and if there is a further drop in the CPI to a figure 11 percent below the initial base, the pension is reduced by 1 percent.

Two restrictions also apply to these adjustments. First, no semiannual change can be more than 5 percent of the amount previously payable. Second, no increase can be made such that the relative rise in the initial pension amount exceeds 7½ percent times the number of years that the individual has been on the pension roll.

The National Airlines plan for management employees has never had the CPI-adjusted earnings record basis because it is a final-average-pay plan (last five years). Pensions in force under this plan are adjusted in the same manner as under the plans for pilots and communications employees, with one exception; any increase in pension under the plan, measured from the date of retirement, has offset against it the increase in the social security primary benefit over the same period (except that this will not be allowed to cause the pension under the plan to decrease if the CPI had not declined in the period since the last adjustment).

The National Airlines plans for employees other than pilots, communications employees, and management employees do not contain automatic-adjustment provisions for pensions in course of payment.

The Bankers Trust Company (New York) has studied corporate pension plans in depth for almost 40 years and has issued ten comprehensive reports summarizing the provisions of a large number of such plans. It is significant to note that not until in the most recent report (1975) was any detailed analysis given to the subject of benefit increases for pensioners.

This Bankers Trust study involved 271 corporate pension plans (190 different employers), with the total number of employees covered amounting to 8.4 million. About 75 percent of these plans were of the conventional type, and the remainder were of the pattern type (i.e., a form of plan adopted by certain international unions which has been negotiated, with minor variations, with different employers). Although in recent years, many of the pension plans provided ad hoc increases for pensioners on the roll, only 8 out of the 271 plans (or 3.0 percent) contained automatic-adjustment provisions. A number of plans do provide variable pensions after retirement based on the performance of an equity portfolio, but this does not fall within the meaning of automatic adjustments.

The eight plans with automatic adjustments for pensions in force tended to be concentrated in certain industries—four of them were life insurance companies, two were utilities, and the other two were aerospace and a container manufacturer (the only bargained plan, which will be discussed in more detail later). Based on the information available, all of these plans had adopted the automatic-adjustment provisions in the 1970s.

The four plans of life insurance companies were quite similar and will be discussed later in connection with a special study that was made with regard to this business. The aerospace plan has an annual adjustment each March (either up or down, but with a floor of the original amount at time of retirement) according to the change in the CPI for the previous calendar year as against that for the second preceding year, but with a 3 percent maximum annual increase.

One of the utility plans increases pensions on the roll if the CPI changes by at least ½ percent, but there is a 2 percent maximum annual increase (on a cumulative basis, so that increases not recognized in previous years will be recognized in future years if the CPI does not rise sufficiently to use up the 2 percent maximum). Under the other utility plan, after there is a change in the CPI of at least 20 percent, pensions in force are increased by 80 percent of the CPI rise, with a maximum increase in the monthly pension of $100 and a minimum increase of $10 (but no increase at all if the result comes out less than $5).

The Conference Board (New York) has made several surveys of personnel practices in the benefits and times-off-with-pay areas for private business and industry. The latest survey was made as of late 1972 and 1973 and; as to employee benefits, included 1,601 concerns in various types of businesses (both small and large firms, although employing at least 250 persons in every case).[3] Only 3.9 percent of the pension plans for managerial employees provided for automatic adjustment of pensions in force according to changes in the CPI. This proportion was almost as high for plans covering other office employees (3.7 percent), but was notably lower for plans covering nonoffice employees (2.4 percent). Table 12 gives more details on this subject and shows that indexing of pensions is most prevalent in plans of insurance companies and electric and gas utilities and to some extent in medium-sized manufacturing and commercial banking.

Another source of information about the prevalence of indexing provisions for pensions in course of payment under private pension

---

[3] Mitchell Meyer and Harland Fox, *Profile of Employee Benefits* (New York: The Conference Board, 1974). Through the courtesy of the authors, certain unpublished data underlying this study was made available to the author and is presented here.

TABLE 12

Proportion of Pension Plans with Provisions for Automatic Adjustment of Pensions in Course of Payment, by Type of Business, Survey by the Conference Board, 1972–1973

Type of Business	Managerial Employees		Other Office Employees		Nonoffice Employees	
	Number of Plans Reported	Proportion with Automatic Adjustment	Number of Plans Reported	Proportion with Automatic Adjustment	Number of Plans Reported	Proportion with Automatic Adjustment
Commercial banking ...	313	4.2%	313	3.8%	—	—
Insurance	223	8.5	227	8.4	—	—
Large manufacturing ...	487	1.2	483	1.2	472	1.3%
Medium manufacturing	62	3.2	60	3.3	63	4.8
Electric and gas utilities	114	7.0	114	7.0	110	6.4
Retail and wholesale trade	76	2.6	76	2.6	72	1.4
Construction	13	0.0	14	0.0	3	0.0
Trucking	21	0.0	23	0.0	19	5.3
Hotel and restaurant service	10	10.0	11	0.0	8	0.0
Air transportation	14	7.1	14	0.0	14	0.0
Total	1,333	3.9%	1,335	3.7%	761	2.4%

plans is the annual survey of employee benefits (noncash compensation) made by Hay-Huggins, Consulting Actuaries (Philadelphia). The mid-1977 survey included 431 participating employers who had pension plans (276 industrial firms and 155 financial and service firms) and indicated—as do the other data available on this subject—that relatively few private pension plans contain such indexing provisions (see Table 13). However, this survey, which is the most recent one, showed a higher proportion of plans with such provisions (7.3 percent) than did the others, and also somewhat higher maximum limitations on the percentage increase per year (44 percent of the plans with adjustments based on the CPI had a maximum in excess of 3 percent).

The Hay-Huggins survey also showed a number of interesting matters with regard to automatic adjustment of pensions in course of payment that were not mentioned in other surveys. Three plans have routine or guaranteed increases, not dependent on CPI changes. Six of the 25 plans with adjustment based on the CPI increase pensions by only a part of the CPI rise. All plans indexing by the CPI have a maximum-increase provision, almost always on

TABLE 13
Proportion of Pension Plans with Provisions for Automatic Adjustment of Pensions in Course of Payment, by Type of Business, Survey by Hay-Huggins, Mid-1977

Type of Adjustment	Industrial	Financial and Services	Total
	Type of Firm		
	Number (and Percentage) with Automatic Adjustment		
Total reporting	269	155	424*
With automatic adjustment	14 (5%)	17 (11%)	31 (7%)
By constant percent†	—	3	3
Based on CPI‡	12	13	25
Other basis	2	1	3
	Number Adjusting by CPI, according to Annual Maximum Increase		
Total................................	12	13	25
1.5% maximum	1	—	1
2% maximum	2	2	4
3% maximum	3	5	8
4% maximum	1	3	4
4.2% maximum	—	1	1
5% maximum	4	2	6
Dollar maximum§	1	—	1

   * Seven plans did not respond to this matter.

   † This percentage was 1 percent in one plan and 3 percent in the other two plans.

   ‡ Six plans (two industrial and four financial and services) increased pensions by only part of the CPI rise.

   § One plan had only a dollar maximum, while two plans had both a dollar maximum and a maximum percentage increase. These dollar maximum on the increase in monthly pension were $20.00, $20.83, and $31.50.

a percentage-increase-per-year basis (ranging from 1½ percent per year to 3 percent). In ten plans, a minimum increase in the CPI is required to trigger an adjustment (generally, 1 or 3 percent). In about two thirds of the plans, decreases in the CPI result in reduction of the pension (although, undoubtedly, never below the initial amount).

The life insurance business reports each year on various aspects of the pension plans that it administers (in a series of reports entitled *Pension Facts*, issued by the American Council of Life Insurance). As of the end of 1976, there were 38,150 such plans (with 1,091,180 persons covered) that were on the variable-annuity basis using equity investments and 310 such plans (with 245,550 persons covered) that adjusted pensions in course of payment by the CPI or some other index. No details are available on the 310 plans with automatic-adjustment provisions, but it is believed that in a substantial proportion of the cases, they relate to employees of insurance companies (and this is especially so as to numbers of persons covered).

A special study of indexing of pensions in force under retirement plans for employees of life insurance companies has been published by the Life Office Management Association (*Survey on Pension Adjustments for Retirees,* conducted by the Ohio National Life Insurance Company, Spring 1975). The survey was made among the 40 largest mutual companies and the 35 largest stock companies in the United States (of whom 39 and 30, respectively, responded). The companies with pension plans providing for automatic adjustment of benefits in force numbered 15 (10 mutual and 5 stock companies), or 22 percent of the total respondents. All such plans have a maximum increase, with such cap being 4 percent in one plan, 3 percent in 11 plans, and 2 percent in 3 plans. On the basis of the Bankers Trust study, it would seem that there is a general pattern among the pension plans of insurance companies, such that the adjustment can be down as well as up (but with a floor of the original pension amount) and that the CPI change is measured from the second preceding calendar year to the preceding one.

There appear to be only a few collectively bargained pension plans in the United States that have contained automatic-adjustment features for benefits in force. The major instance occurred in 1974 when the United Steelworkers of America made efforts to include such a provision in its agreement with the major aluminum companies and later with the major can companies. The provision that was agreed to in collective bargaining for the aluminum companies was that retirees after January 1974 would receive automatic adjustments for February of 1976 and 1977 on the basis of 65 percent of the increase in the CPI for the preceding calendar year as against the second preceding one. The factor of 65 percent was apparently without any theoretical justification, being the result of collective bargaining. The agreement with the can companies was similar to that for the aluminum companies, except that it applied for only one increase (for March 1976). In the collective bargaining in 1977, these indexing provisions were not renewed as to future changes in the CPI, but any increases that had been made were continued for the lifetime of the retirees.

Two other examples of automatic adjustments of pensions in force in collectively bargained plans are in plans negotiated by the Amalgamated Transit Union, AFL-CIO. In 1966 the plan in the Washington, D.C., transit system (then a private company, but now a governmental entity as an interstate instrumentality) introduced a provision under which pensions in force are automatically adjusted according to changes in the level of wages of the active work force (actually, on the basis of the wage rate of the top-rated vehicle operator), with decreases being possible, but not to the extent of reducing the pension below its initial amount. Effective for 1975, the plan in the Richmond, Virginia, transit system initiated an escalator provision based on the CPI, with maximum annual changes of 4 percent being allowed and with decreases being possible (but not below the initial pension amount); any changes beyond the 4 percent limit are accumulated as credits (or debits, as the case may be) applicable to future changes.

Nonprofit organizations in the charitable, educational, and religious fields have perhaps been more active in introducing variable-pension features than private business organizations. Undoubtedly, the best-known instance is the conglomeration of pension plans for about 500,000 employees of educational and research institutions which are administered by Teachers Insurance and Annuity Association and its affiliate, College Retirement Equities Fund. The CREF portion is a variable-annuity arrangement, based on common stock investments. These plans are, of course, not of the automatic-adjustment type involved in this study.

The National Health and Welfare Retirement Association operates somewhat in the same manner as TIAA-CREF but in the field of nonprofit organizations of a health or welfare nature. Among the various types of plans that such employing organizations can purchase from NHWRA is one that went into effect in 1974, under which the initial pension amount is based on final salary (highest five consecutive years in the last ten years); at the option of the employer, an automatic cost-of-living supplement can be provided. The adjustment applies only after age 65 and is made each May on the basis of the increase in the CPI for the preceding December as compared with the second preceding December, rounded to the nearest 0.1 percent. No change is made if the rise is less than 1 percent (and thus no decreases can occur), and under those circumstances, the base month for measuring the CPI increase remains unchanged. The maximum increase allowable is 4 percent per year (unless the Board of Trustees of NHWRA votes a higher amount). Pro rata increases are given to those who had not been on the pension roll for the full year before the increase becomes payable. As of May 1978, 118 employers with about 3,700 active employees had adopted this provision; such employers represented about 11 percent of the total number of employers who had such a final-pay pension plan and could have elected to provide such a feature.

An interesting automatic-adjustment provision applicable to pensions in course of payment in a retirement plan of a nonprofit organization was that adopted by the Rockefeller Foundation (New York), effective in 1976.[4] Each January, pension amounts are automatically increased by the rise in the CPI between the second preceding September and the preceding September. No decreases are made; if the CPI drops between Septembers, the next base point is the later September—not the earlier one, when the CPI was higher. An important limitation on the amount of the increase is based on the prime interest rate.[5] If the adjustment based on the CPI change is 4 percent or less, it is made without limitation. On the other hand, when the CPI change exceeds 4 percent, then the smaller of that change or the excess of the average prime interest rate for the 12-month period ending the previous September over 3 percent is applicable.[6] For example, if the CPI increase is 7 percent, and the average prime interest rate is 8 percent (as it was during February, March, and April 1978), then the adjustment would be 5 percent (note that as long as the prime rate is 7 percent or less—as it was in 1976 and the first eight months of 1977—the adjustment cannot exceed 4 percent per year).

A logical theory underlies the approach taken in the Rockefeller Foundation plan—namely, that the adjustment should (conservatively) be based on the excess of the short-term interest rate over

---

[4] For a brief description, see Herbert Heaton, "An Indexed Pension Plan at Low Cost," *Pension World,* September 1975. Mr. Heaton, comptroller of the Rockefeller Foundation, kindly made available to the author the full plan description.

[5] Based on the "average prime rate charged by banks," as published in monthly issues of *Business Conditions Digest,* issued by the Bureau of Economic Analysis, U.S. Department of Commerce.

[6] For those who, in January, have been on the roll for less than 12 months, a pro rata portion of the adjustment is payable.

the "true" or "real" interest rate, but should (from a social adequacy standpoint) be at least 4 percent per year. It was estimated that for the period 1955–74, this procedure would have increased pension amounts by about 90 percent of what would have occurred under a straight CPI basis with no limit.

Retirement plans established by church denominations for their ministers and lay employees sometimes embody the variable-annuity principle based on investment in equities. In only one instance, however, does such a plan contain an automatic-adjustment provision for pensions in course of payment. The United Methodist Church has a pension plan for personnel of its general boards and agencies which, beginning in 1974, provides for annual adjustments in Januarys based on the CPI change from the second preceding June to the preceding one. The adjustment is applicable only to pensions that have been in force for at least one year. Decreases, as well as increases, are possible, but with a floor of the initial pension amount.

None of the survey data on automatic-adjustment provisions in private pension plans in the United States indicated the presence of any that did so either by routine or guaranteed percentage increases regardless of CPI changes or by increases in the salaries of the active work force. For several years, two denominational pension plans (Lutheran Church in America and Southern Baptist Convention) have made available, as an option, a guaranteed increasing-pension basis. The only such procedure that the author has run across in the pension plan of a private employer is that instituted by a prominent actuarial consulting firm in 1977 in the plan for its own employees. In all three instances, the increases are on a compound basis, rather than on a simple-increase basis as are the governmental plans which follow this practice.

Almost invariably, it seems to be the case under private pension plans in the United States that automatic-adjustment provisions do not apply to vested deferred pensions during the period of deferment. There is somewhat of an exception to this general procedure in defined-contribution (money-purchase) plans, like TIAA-CREF and denominational pension plans, under which those with vested deferred pension rights do receive the advantage of excess investment earnings over the "guaranteed interest rate" during the period of deferment. Another exception is in the case of the defined-benefit plans for both the United Presbyterian Church in the U.S.A. and the Presbyterian Church in the United States, under which those with vested deferred pensions share in any favorable investment experience.

The plan for employees of the several Federal Reserve banks throughout the country provides the same increase rates (which have in the past closely approximated the changes in the CPI, although not being automatic, but rather noncontractual) for persons eligible for early retirement at reduced pension amounts but deferring receipt of pension to a later age as for pensions in course of payment. This, however, may be said to be only actuarially equitable, and not true automatic adjustment of vested deferred pensions available only at a later date.

INDEXING IN PRIVATE PENSION PLANS IN CANADA

Just as in the United States—and perhaps to an even greater extent—governmental pension plans in Canada (both social security and for government employees) often contain indexing provisions for pensions in course of payment. Similarly, in both countries, such provisions are relatively infrequent in pension plans in the private sector.

One impediment in Canadian corporate tax law had formerly hampered the adoption of such provisions. There had been a prohibition against funding in advance the anticipated cost thereof (or, rather, any such expenditures could not be counted as a business cost for income tax purposes). In 1975, this restriction was eliminated, subject to the limitation that the assumed rate of CPI increase must be at least two percentage points lower than the assumed interest rate, which certainly seems to be a reasonable, consistent relationship.

Summary data on pension plans in Canada is collected by the federal government and has been published for 1970 and 1974.[7] The 1974 data are shown in Table 14 and bring out quite clearly the relative small extent of escalator provisions based on changes in the CPI contained in pension plans in the private sector—only 1 percent of the plans and 2 percent of the members. In 1970, only 60 plans with 191,700 members contained such provisions (17 public-sector plans with 175,783 employees and 43 private-sector plans

---

[7] *Pension Plans in Canada, 1970* and *Pension Plans in Canada, 1974,* Statistics Canada, Information Canada, Ottawa (October 1972 and April 1976).

TABLE 14
Prevalence of Provisions for Indexing Pensions in Course of Payment in Canada, 1974

Sector	Total Plans	Plans with Indexing Provision		Plans with Indexing with No Maximum	
		Number	Percent of Total	Number	Percentage of Total with Indexing
		By Number of Plans			
Public	751	40	5.3%	*	*
Private	15,102	101	0.7	*	*
Total ..	15,853	141	0.9	10	7.1%
		By Number of Plan Members			
Public	1,480,103	566,334	38.3%	*	*
Private	1,944,142	41,560	2.1	*	*
Total ..	3,424,245	607,894	17.8	502,500	82.7%

* Data not available.
Note: As discussed in Chapter 6, since 1974 there has been a great increase in the extent of indexing provisions in public-sector plans. Apparently, however, this has not occurred in private-sector plans.
Source: *Pension Plans in Canada, 1974,* Statistics Canada, Information Canada, April 1976.

with only 15,917 employees). As discussed in Chapter 6, since 1974 there has been a great increase in the extent of indexing provisions in public-sector plans. Apparently, however, this has not occurred in private-sector plans.

In general, pension plans in the private sector which provide automatic adjustment for pensions in course of payment for changes in the CPI have a maximum or cap on the amount of relative annual increase—generally 2 or 3 percent. For example, Bell Canada updates every five years and has a cap of 10 percent. A quite liberal plan is that of Shell Canada, with annual updating and a 10 percent cap.

A method used by a few plans (e.g., the Toronto Transit Commission Pension Fund Society) is to increase the pensions in course of payment on the basis of the investment experience of its fixed-interest securities. Specifically, the pensions are increased each year by the excess of the actual rate of return (usually, averaged over a period of a few years) over the interest rate used in the actuarial valuation. Such increases can be permanent and guaranteed (ignoring the matter of whether actual mortality is the same as the tabular mortality in the valuation) because when excess interest rate is applied to augment the pension reserves, this merely means that such reserves can finance pensions that are much larger percentage-wise.

Periodic surveys of employee remuneration in Canada are made by Hay Associates (paralleling the surveys for the United States made by Hay-Huggins, as discussed previously). The survey as of the summer of 1977 covered 155 organizations—114 industrial firms, 31 finance firms (including 10 life insurance companies), and 10 nonprofit organizations. Only 13 percent of the plans have automatic-adjustment provisions applicable to pensions in course of payment (as compared with 10 percent in the 1975 survey). For those plans with automatics, the adjustments are based on the CPI or the CPP/QPP Pension Index in all but about 10 percent of the cases in both the 1975 and 1977 surveys; when adjustment is based on such indexes, the full extent of the rise is recognized in as many as 94 percent of the plans in 1977 (but as few as 70 percent in 1975). As to limitations on the size of the increase under the escalation provisions, 67 percent of the plans in 1977 (70 percent in 1975) contain such a provision, usually with a 2 or 3 percent annual maximum.

In 1977, the Canadian government had a survey made by an actuarial consulting firm as to the extent of adjustments of benefit amounts in private pension plans. This was part of an overall study of the pension plans for federal employees that was made, in large part, as a result of public concern over the liberality of such plans as compared with those for employees in the private sector (as mentioned in Chapter 7). This study is entitled "Report on the Financing of the Pensions of Federal Public Service Employees," Tomenson-Alexander Associates (Toronto), November 30, 1977.

The Tomenson-Alexander report made a study of 149 plans of companies with 500 or more employees (out of a total of about 600 in the country); these plans covered 460,235 members. Thirteen plans (with 68,163 members) had automatic-adjustment provisions related to the CPI applicable to pensions in course of payment. One plan (with 1,078 members) increased pensions by the investment earnings on the fund applicable to pensioners in excess of the amount "required" by the valuation interest rate. Another two plans (with 3,744 members) provided routine automatic increases by either a fixed dollar amount or a fixed percentage.

The 16 plans with automatic-adjustment provisions represented

11 percent of all plans surveyed in the Tomenson-Alexander study. At the same time, the 72,985 employees covered under such plans with escalation provisions represented 16 percent of the total employees under all plans in the study. It was estimated that the vast majority of participants in plans providing automatic adjustments were in plans which contained a cap on the annual increase of less than 4 percent, such proportion being about 80 percent. Besides the 11 percent of the plans with automatics, a further 68 percent of all plans had made ad hoc adjustments of pensions in course of payment. In these approximately 80 percent of all plans which had either automatic or ad hoc adjustments, the level thereof approximated 66 percent of the change in the CPI during 1971–75.

In early 1978, the government of Quebec released a report of an advisory group (the so-called "Confirentes" committee) dealing with recommendations in the area of private pension plans. In the field of indexing, it was recommended that all investment earnings above those based on the valuation interest rate should be used for up-dating of benefits, both before and after retirement. Further, it was recommended that the valuation interest rate utilized should not exceed a rate to be established by the Quebec Pension Board, which would likely be the real rate of return in the economy (i.e., about 3 percent). The theory thus apparently is that "excess" investment returns resulting from inflation should be used to maintain the real value of the benefits.

INDEXING IN PRIVATE PENSION PLANS IN OTHER COUNTRIES[8]

Information about automatic-adjustment provisions for pensions in course of payment in private pension plans outside of North America is relatively sparse. On the whole, such provisions appear to be found only infrequently, and then generally only when required by the government (as in second-tier private plans "required" by law), and do not appear at all in non-European countries.

Retirement plans for government employees outside of North America are, however, much more likely to contain escalation

---

[8] Most of the material in this section is based on information kindly furnished by John K. Dyer, Jr., F.S.A., or from the International Benefits Information Service (of which Mr. Dyer is an editor).

provisions (in some instances, not on a "guaranteed" automatic basis, but rather by custom) for pensions in course of payment than private pension plans in those countries. Such, for example, are found for the retirement systems of employees of the central governments of Austria, France, Ireland, Italy, Norway, Switzerland, and the United Kingdom. The adjustment is on the basis of changes in the salary levels of active employees in the Austrian, French, Irish, and Norwegian plans and on the basis of price changes in the Italian, Swiss, and United Kingdom plans.

In Austria, Belgium, Denmark, Ireland, Norway, and Sweden, the practice has been followed under pension plans administered by insurance companies to grant pension increases from profits returned to the employer-policyholder (in the form of dividends or paid-up additions). Moreover, in Belgium this procedure is required under tax law with respect to profits arising from employer contributions.

Private pension plans in the Federal Republic of Germany (West) adjust pensions in course of payment only by ad hoc methods or through dividend additions, and not by automatic escalators. Legislation in 1974 provided that all employers must review the level of their pensions in force every three years as to their adequacy, and this must be done independently of the governmental social insurance benefits (so that any increases therein are not to be considered). Conceivably, this could lead to some automatic formula for pension adjustments. At present, however, the requirement is considered to be fulfilled if the adjustment is at least 50 percent of the increase in the cost-of-living index for a four-person family.

France has several nationwide pension plans which supplement its social security system. Three of these are those for manual and clerical workers, for supervisors and lower level executives, and for senior executives. In essence, by collective bargaining and by law, these "private" pension plans could well be considered to be governmental social insurance programs. Both earnings records used in determining initial pension amounts and pensions in course of payment are indexed in a rather complex manner.[9] The systems are financed on essentially a pay-as-you-go basis. It is intended that the adjustments to pensions in course of payment should keep them

---

[9] For more details of this program, see J. R. Trowbridge, "Assessmentism—An Alternative to Pensions Funding," *Journal of the Institute of Actuaries,* London, vol. 104 (1977).

in pace with the cost of living, if sufficient financing results from the indexing of the taxable wage base (or otherwise).

Finland, too, has mandatory private pension plans supplementing its social security system. In addition, there is a third tier of voluntary additional private pensions. Both sets of private pension plans are administered by insurance companies. The pensions in course of payment are automatically adjusted for changes in both wages and the cost of living (with equal weight being given to the two indexes).

In Switzerland, it has been proposed that all employers be required to provide pensions supplementing social security benefits. Contributions to a pooled fund would be required, and such fund would be intended to provide, among other things, for adjustments to pensions in course of payment for changes in the price level. A somewhat similar proposal has been made in the Netherlands, but it has not been as actively considered as that in Switzerland.

The United Kingdom has a two-tier social security system providing pensions. The first tier is universal flat benefits, and the second tier has earnings-related benefits. An employer can opt out of the second tier if there is provided a suitable private pension plan. Among other things, such a private plan must update both the earnings record according to changes in wages and the pensions in course of payment according to price changes. The employer must meet the cost of updating before the pension commences, but the government pays for the escalation costs after retirement. Indexing for price or wage changes is seldom done in British pension plans supplementary to the governmental second-tier plan.

Indexing of Benefits in Pension Plans of International Governmental Organizations

International governmental organizations, just as national ones, almost always establish quite adequate pension plans for their employees. The general philosophy of such organizations in all of the aspects of personnel policy is that their practices should be comparable with the best ones of national governments, especially that in the country where they are located. As a result, automatic adjustment of pensions in force is widespread among pension plans for the staff of international governmental organizations.

Such indexing provisions contain some interesting and unusual procedures. In large part, this is due to the unique characteristics of the employees involved, in that they are generally citizens of various different countries and tend to return home upon retirement. Further, some international organizations have their staff at duty stations in several countries, with their pay being in different currencies. Thus, in a particular plan, not only are there problems in maintaining the purchasing power of pensions in force for retirees in various countries (or when they move between countries) but also in dealing with relative currency adjustments among nations.

This chapter will describe the provisions for automatic adjustment of pensions in force in the retirement plans of a number of international governmental organizations.

UNITED NATIONS

The largest international governmental organization is, of course, the United Nations and its affiliated specialized agencies (such as the Food and Agricultural Organization, International Labor Office, and World Health Organization) if they elect to join and agree to adopt the UN salary system. At present, 11 such specialized agencies plus the International Atomic Energy Agency cover their employees in the United Nations Joint Staff Pension Fund.

First, it is necessary to describe the UN salary system. The professional staff (including those at the highest executive levels) have a uniform worldwide salary scale, varying by position grade and length of service in grade, expressed in U.S. dollars. To this base salary for professionals are added so-called post adjustments to reflect differences in the cost of living at the various duty stations around the world, and also certain allowances for dependents. These base salaries and their supplements are normally not subject to national income taxes. A notional, gross salary is determined for each base salary to reflect the effect of national income taxes (at roughly the average level for seven countries—Austria, Canada, France, Italy, Switzerland, United Kingdom, and United States); this gross salary is used essentially for budgetary purposes. Such gross salary (which, in essence, is the base salary, plus post adjustments, plus average income taxes for that pay level) is also used for purposes of determining pensionable remuneration. (The individual does not receive this gross salary but rather a base salary, plus adjustments, plus amounts needed to pay national and local income taxes when the base salary is not exempt therefrom—as in the United States.) The pensionable remuneration is the gross salary increased by the rise in the average worldwide post-adjustment index from the time that the salary scale was adopted to a recent period before that to which the salary relates (such increases being only in units of full 5 percent rises).

For general service staff (i.e., all employees other than the professional staff), the salaries are based on the "best-prevailing wages" in local currency for the particular position among other employers at the duty station. Once again, the actual salaries are converted to gross salaries, and these are used as pensionable remuneration. Any changes in local living costs are, of course, reflected by changes in the "best-prevailing wages." The pensionable remuneration is considered in terms of U.S. dollars, with each month's salary being converted from the currency of the duty station at the going rate of exchange. Similarly, the pensions were—until recently—paid in U.S. dollars (or else converted into other currencies at the going rate of exchange).

This procedure worked out very satisfactorily as far as the members and pensioners were concerned so long as the U.S. dollar was as strong as any other currency (and more so than most). The pensioners still had problems with the generally slowly rising cost of living and thus the loss of purchasing power of the pension. However, the problem was greatly enlarged for some pensioners (primarily those in Switzerland and other central and northern European nations) when the U.S. dollar was devalued or otherwise depreciated relative to some currencies beginning in 1971.[1] And at the same time that such pensioners were getting fewer units of their local currency per dollar of their pension check, the cost of living in their country was rising.

It may be of interest to give the developments that occurred in the past in connection with the present provisions for automatically adjusting the pensions in course of payment in the UN plan. In 1960 the Pension Review Group, which was a body of outside experts established to make a comprehensive review of the plan, recommended that in view of the small, but steady, worldwide inflation in recent years, an automatic increase in pensions of 1 percent annually, without regard to actual price changes in individual countries where pensioners are resident, should be provided. The Pension Review Group believed that adjustment on any other basis would be too complicated and would possibly have serious cost implications. It also opposed converting the pension at time of retirement into the currency of the retiree's home country because of the possible cost problems for the fund and the investment difficulties that might be involved. The annual adjustment of 1 percent was adopted, effective in 1962.

In 1965, however, an automatic-adjustment basis related to price changes was adopted for pensions in course of payment. Its general

---

[1] For example, the U.S. dollar fell by about 45 percent as against the Swiss franc from April 1971 to mid-1977. Similar declines occurred against other currencies, such as the West German mark (37 percent), Netherlands guilder (32 percent), Belgian franc (29 percent), Danish kroner (18 percent), and French franc (11 percent). On the other hand, the U.S. dollar appreciated against some currencies, such as the Italian lira (41 percent), British pound (38 percent), Indian rupee (14 percent), Canadian dollar (6 percent), and Australian dollar (1 percent).

basis was indexing for changes (either up or down, but not below the initial amount) in the average worldwide (in duty stations of UN staff) cost of living, through the use of a weighted average of post adjustments (WAPA), the same data as used for adjusting pensionable remuneration. The post adjustments were expressed as an index (1958 equaling 100).

For a particular retiree, the base pension adjustment index was the average of the post-adjustment indexes for the five years preceding the year of retirement. Each subsequent year, the pension adjustment index for the individual is computed as the average of the post-adjustment index for the preceding five years. The percentage increase of the current pension adjustment index over the base pension adjustment index (rounded to the nearest percent) was applied to the original pension amount (in U.S. dollars).

A five-year averaging period was used in order to be consistent with the average salary for pension computation purposes, which was based on the last five years of service. Such use of a five-year averaging period was to prevent the adjustments from out-running the rate of accumulation of the same cost-of-living element in new pensions granted, with the intention of keeping both new and continuing pensions approximately consistent. Subsequently, both such periods were changed to three years. The WAPA system was never on a permanent basis as a provision of the plan, but rather it has been periodically extended by the General Assembly, usually for three-year periods.

The procedure of using price indexing based on several past years' data would have no different effect than using only a recent short period if the trend of price changes is at a uniform percentage rate annually.[2] However, if prices rise at a rapidly increasing rate (as they did in the early 1970s), the pension adjustment lags behind price changes (although later when the latter level off, the pension adjustments catch up). In fact, if the rate of increase in prices is decreasing, the pension adjustments exceed the price changes.

An example will perhaps clarify the situation. If the post-adjustment indexes for the five years preceding retirement were 110, 112,

---

[2] For example, if the cost of living increases by X percent per year, and if the index is 100 in the fifth year before retirement, then the adjustment n years after the year of retirement is:

$$[100 (y^n + y^{n+1} + y^{n+2} + y^{n+3} + y^{n+4}) \div 100 (1 + y + y^2 + y^3 + y^4)],$$

where $y = 1 + 0.01X$. This term simplifies to y^n, which is the same factor as would be used if the adjustment were based on only a one-year period (or even a one-month period).

116, 120, and 127, respectively, then the base pension adjustment index for the individual is 117. If the postadjustment index for the year of retirement is 140, then the pension adjustment index applicable for this individual for the year after the year of retirement is 123 (the average of 112, 116, 120, 127, and 140), or a relative increase of 5 percent. If the person had retired at the beginning of the year, the pension for the next year would be increased by 5 percent (proportionately less for those retiring at later points during the year). It will be observed that such increase is well below the increase in the post-adjustment index as measured over a one-year period (10.2 percent).

The WAPA system became quite unpopular with the participants and pensioners in the early 1970s because of the rapid increase in prices then and also for those in the European countries, whose currencies appreciated so significantly against the U.S. dollar, because of the decrease in the pension amounts in their local currency equivalent. As a result, several ad hoc increases (applicable to pensioners in all countries) were made. There was considerable demand for selective adjustment of pensions to recognize the country of residence of the retiree, especially due to the effect of monetary revaluations upward, but the principle of universality of treatment was nonetheless retained.

As a result, in 1975, a new basis of adjustment of pensions in course of payment under the UN plan was adopted. Two alternatives are available to the beneficiaries. They can either stay under the WAPA system (which maintains the universality principle), or they can elect a new CPI system (under which the adjustment is selective—according to the country of residence). A switch to the CPI system is possible at any time. This dual WAPA-CPI system, too, was enacted on a temporary basis, subject to renewal (now being applicable through 1978).

The General Assembly of the UN, however, was not satisfied with the dual system as a permanent measure because of the difficulties for the participants in making a choice (which could turn out wrong) and because of the resulting uncertainties as to the costs involved to the plan. Therefore, it directed that an adjustment procedure should be developed that (1) would be on a unified (or single) and durable basis and (2) could be financed without increasing the cost of the present system of benefits (including the adjustment provision).

The board of the UN pension plan did develop a unified basis in 1976 for the adjustment of pensions in course of payment. Under this approach, the dual WAPA-CPI system would be eliminated for retirements in the future.

For professional staff, the initial pension would be calculated first in U.S. dollars and then would be converted permanently into the currency of the country of retirement by the application of an "exchange rate." Such rate would be derived from the relationship of (*a*) the actual salary plus post-adjustment payable in local currency in that country for a particular job level to (*b*) the corresponding U.S. dollar salary and post-adjustment payable for employment in New York City. However, if conversion of the initial pension in U.S. dollars into local currency at the current open-market currency exchange rate would produce a higher local-currency amount, then the pension would be established at that figure. The latter alternative would generally be applicable in countries which are of a low-cost character (i.e., usually most non-European ones).

Adjustments after retirement for professional staff would be on the basis of the changes in the CPI of the country of retirement, except when the conversion had been made at the current open-market currency exchange rate. In the latter circumstances, the adjustment would be on the basis of changes in the U.S. CPI. An alternative clause would, nevertheless, provide that if the first conversion method (an exchange rate based on local versus New York remuneration, plus adjustment on the basis of the local CPI) proved subsequently to be more advantageous for a pensioner for whom the second conversion method (current open-market currency exchange rate initially, plus adjustment on the basis of the U.S. CPI) had been used, then the adjustment thereafter would be determined on such first method.

For general service staff, the procedure would be somewhat different. For those retiring in the country of their last duty station (for this category, by far the most typical situation), the pension in U.S. dollars would be converted to the local currency (using the average rate of exchange in the three years prior to separation); thereafter, the pension amount would be adjusted by changes in the local consumer price index. For those relatively few in this category who retire to a different country than that of the last duty station, the initial pension would be computed in the same manner as for professional staff, using for conversion purposes, however, the more favorable of (a) relationship between the actual salary plus post adjustment of the country of retirement and that of the country of last duty station or (b) current open-market rate of exchange between the U.S. dollar and the currency of the country of retirement. Subsequent adjustment would be on the basis of the CPI in the country of retirement (but with the same savings clause as for professional staff).

This proposal was not accepted by the General Assembly when it considered the matter in late 1976. Instead, the board of the UN plan was directed to make further studies, with the admonition that "the principle of compensating by whatever means for country-to-country differences in the cost of living should be given limited recognition falling short of equality of purchasing power so, as to ensure that the new scheme does not require an increase in the present or future financial liabilities of Member States."

As a result, in early 1978 the standing committee of the board of the UN plan developed a new, interesting approach. The proposed adjustment system would provide that the pension amount would not be allowed to fall below the real value of its statutory U.S. dollar amount, while at the same time having its purchasing power being preserved as initially established in the currency of the beneficiary's country of residence. Thus, the beneficiary would receive each month the larger of (1) the initial pension amount in U.S. dollars increased by changes in the U.S. CPI (and converted into local currency at the then-prevailing rate of exchange) or (2) the initial pension amount converted into local currency as of the effective time of award of the pension (at the more favorable— to the beneficiary— of [a] the rate of exchange on the date of award or [b] the average of such rates for the preceding 36 months).

All in all, it can be seen that developing an equitable, consistent adjustment system is extremely difficult, if not really impossible. This is so because of the problems of varying rates of price changes in different nations and the possibilities of currency devaluations or revaluations. Another problem in maintaining equality of purchasing power of UN pensions as among retirees in different countries is the diverse income tax provisions of various nations.[3] This prob-

---

[3] Some countries (such as Austria) completely exempt UN pensions from income tax. Also, some nations finance extensive social benefit programs through high income taxes, whereas others do so by earmarked taxes or through general revenues derived from sales taxes (or similar ones).

lem has been recognized, but so far no serious consideration has been given to solving it.

ORGANIZATION OF AMERICAN STATES

The Organization of American States has employees from the various American countries, who are employed mainly in Washington, D.C., although there are a number of other duty stations throughout the two continents. The benefits are determined in U.S. dollars, and the automatic-adjustment provisions for pensions in course of payment are based on changes in the CPI for the Washington metropolitan area, regardless of the nationality or residence of the beneficiary.

Problems have not arisen on this account, as they did in the United Nations pension plan, because to date the U.S. dollar has been relatively more stable than virtually all other American currencies, so that the beneficiaries have been content with this procedure. Moreover, this pension plan permits complete commutation of benefits at retirement, so that individuals who do not like the indexing procedure could take this way out (and, in fact, most have done so).

INTER-AMERICAN DEVELOPMENT BANK

The Inter-American Development Bank, located in Washington, D.C., has somewhat the same situation as the Organization of American States with regard to the citizenship and location of its employees. It, too, has adopted the approach of automatic adjustment of pensions in force according to changes in the CPI for the Washington metropolitan area. The increases are on a guaranteed basis only up to a cumulative amount of 5 percent per year (i.e., with carry-over to subsequent years of any unused amount in a particular year). However, upon approval by the governing authorities, this maximum can be exceeded and, in fact, in practice such has been the case in all past years when this situation occurred.

WORLD BANK AND INTERNATIONAL MONETARY FUND

The World Bank and International Monetary Fund are two closely related, although independent, agencies located in Washington, D.C. Their staffs are drawn from various countries throughout the world, but none are employed at any place other than the central office.

Because of the wide range of nations employed, the problem of devaluation of the dollar is present, just as in the United Nations pension plan (although not the problem of employment in various duty stations throughout the world).

These two plans have adopted a relatively simple approach as compared with the several attempts that the United Nations plan has made, because fewer employees are involved, and there is much less wide geographic distribution of their likely eventual residences when they become pensioners. Specifically, the automatic-adjustment provisions under these plans involve a dual choice. The pensioner can take a benefit payable in U.S. dollars, adjusted automatically each year according to changes in the CPI for the Washington metropolitan area (with no maximum limit), or the pensioner can convert the pension in U.S. dollars to the currency of the country of residence, with automatic adjustment according to that country's CPI.

INTERNATIONAL FISHERIES COMMISSIONS

A unified pension system has been established for six North American fisheries commissions that are largely joint between Canada and the United States. The pension plan is administered through an insurance company. In recent years, pensions in force have been adjusted by ad hoc action, which the administering group hope will be continued in the future, and which are financed when the cost emerges by purchasing additional units of annuity. In order to parallel the retirement systems for civil servants in the two countries, the annual pension adjustments are based on the changes in the CPI (either Canadian or United States, depending upon the location of the particular commission), with pro rata adjustments for persons coming on the roll during the preceding year.

INTERNATIONAL ORGANIZATIONS BASED IN EUROPE

Several international organizations which are primarily concerned with European affairs have quite similar automatic-adjustment provisions for pensions in course of payment. Such organizations include the European Economic Community (commonly referred to as the Common Market) and the Organization for Economic Cooperation and Development. The · problems of developing an equitable and rational indexing system for these organizations is not nearly as difficult as for the United Nations because the countries involved, and thus the nationalities of the employees, are relatively few and are more nearly homogeneous in nature from an economic standpoint.

The indexing approach provided is one that is very favorable to the participants. The initial pension amount, as determined by length of service and final average salary in the last country of employment, is converted to the currency of the country of residence of the pensioner and is then adjusted periodically according to the changes in current salary of employees of the same grade and level as the individual was at the time of retirement.

ASIAN DEVELOPMENT BANK

The Asian Development Bank is located in Manila, Republic of the Philippines, and employs a staff that is composed largely of persons from that region of the world. At the inception of the plan, it was thought that the automatic-adjustment provisions for pensions in course of payment might be based on differences in currency values and price changes in the country that the pensioner might choose as a residence, but it was found that this was too complicated, particularly because of the lack of adequate data and the unstable economic conditions in some of the countries involved. Accordingly, the simple approach of a routine or guaranteed increase of 3 percent each year in the pension amount was adopted.

Conclusions and Views

The preceding chapters have presented the various aspects and techniques of indexing pensions in course of payment in a manner intended to be purely factual and objective. This chapter will briefly present the author's views and conclusions on the subject.

In general, it seems socially desirable and justifiable that pensions, whether under social insurance systems or private pension plans, should have their value maintained under circumstances of changing price levels. The only exception to this general principle would be in the unlikely (and unfortunate) event that, over a significantly long period of time, prices rise more rapidly than net take-home wages of the active labor force. Under such circumstances, it would, of course, be most unfair and inequitable to have the pensioner class be treated more favorably than the producers. Barring this situation, the purchasing power of pensions should, in all equity, be maintained notwithstanding the views of some persons who believe that pensioners need relatively less purchasing power as they grow older.

Social insurance programs throughout the world, especially those in economically developed countries, have widely adopted indexing of pensions in course of payment without any limitations. In the United States, a high proportion of pension plans for governmental employees have similarly adopted indexing, although generally with some safeguarding limitations as to the amount of indexing provided. Relatively few private pension plans in the United States have adopted indexing, although it is very significant to note that such action has predominantly been done by life insurance companies, which certainly have the most proficiency in the pension planning area and can recognize the necessity for such action.

Private employers in the United States have been hesitant to move into the field of indexing pensions in course of payment because of the high and uncertain costs likely to be involved. Nonetheless, employers have not been too hesitant about maintaining the real value of initial pension awards by adopting final-salary plans.

It is suggested that private plans should desirably take the next step and provide indexing of pensions in course of payment. For those who are afraid to take the full plunge of doing so without any limitations, it might be desirable for them to "get their feet wet" by instituting indexing with certain limitations. Several alternatives (or a combination thereof) are possible in this respect, such as:

1. Providing a maximum annual adjustment (either cumulative or noncumulative);
2. Recognizing CPI changes only in excess of a prescribed rate;
3. Taking into account only a fraction of the CPI increase;
4. Applying the CPI increase to only the first $X of pension;
5. Basing the increase in pension on the excess of the actual investment return over a static interest rate (such as 3 percent), or using the prime interest rate for this purpose instead of the actual rate of return of the fund.
6. Deferring the first increase in pension for several years after retirement, and then basing it on current CPI rises (rather than on that measured from the date of retirement).
7. Providing for CPI adjustments only up to age 70 (so as to encourage retirements before then, who might otherwise be hesitant to do so, because of the declining purchasing power of the dollar and the possibility of remaining in employment—as a result of the new law prohibiting mandatory retirement before age 70—and thus having rising wages).

A combination approach which does not involve any limitation, but yet has certain cost controls and cost-limiting effects, would be to provide indexing only if the pensioner initially chose to take an actuarially reduced pension of a routine increasing nature. For example, if an individual were eligible for a level pension of $100 per month, this could be converted into an actuarially equivalent pension of about $80 per month that would automatically increase by 3 percent (on a compound basis) at the end of each 12 months. The plan would then provide further increase for any changes in the CPI in excess of 3 percent per year. Such a procedure would, of course, greatly reduce the cost of indexing for the employer and would remove much of the concern about the necessary additional financing.

With such a procedure as that just described (or a procedure involving the more conventional approaches to indexing of pensions in course of payment), there is still the paramount question of the additional financial burden and the possible uncertainty as to its magnitude. The author believes that in the past a considerable number of pension plans have, in essence, had their real costs understated by providing no indexing after retirement even though it is essential to the maintenance of the purposes for which the plan was established—and which was often done anyhow on an ad hoc basis. In particular, the actuarial valuations for plans with no post-retirement indexing have frequently been made on the basis of a relatively high interest rate, such as 5 percent or more. Proper actuarial procedure would be to use a salary scale containing an inflation element (for the general level of wages in the country) that would be consistent with the interest rate used. If such a salary scale were not adopted, then the cost of the plan would be significantly understated.

Nonetheless, even if the salary scale and the interest rate are consistent, the author believes that the cost of the pension plan has, in reality, been understated. The excess interest earnings over a "real" interest rate, such as 3 percent, should not have represented profit to the plan, resulting in lower stated costs, but rather should have been utilized for maintaining the purchasing power of the pensions in force. In other words, the valuation interest rate as it applies to pensions in course of payment should be taken at a figure of about the "real" interest rate, and any excess of the actual rate of return over this amount should be utilized to meet the cost of indexing pensions in course of payment. Quite obviously, for a pension plan to change over to such a procedure would produce a higher cost than had previously been derived. In reality, that cost had been illusorily low. It should be realized that the foregoing remarks are not intended to suggest that a plan liberalization can be "paid for" by a change in actuarial assumptions, but rather that the assumptions used previously threw off actuarial gains that should have been utilized to maintain the underlying purposes of the plan, rather than to reduce its apparent costs.

An easy "out" in the direction of indexing pensions in retirement plans of private employers without involving the uncertainties of possible high costs would be if the federal government were to issue bonds with interest payments and principal geared to changes in the CPI, as a few foreign countries have done. Private pension plans could then fund their reserves for pensioners, at least, with such investments and not have to worry about cost uncertainties in this area. Although there has been some talk about this type of security in the United States, the issuance of such bonds does not seem imminent.

The author believes essentially that indexing of pensions in course of payment is necessary to achieve the intended purposes of the plan and that this can be supported financially by appropriate measures or realizations of the costs actually involved. But beyond this, an argument for moving in this direction is that otherwise the federal government may compel it. Once again, it is the old question of a vacuum existing for any length of time ultimately being filled by governmental action. Senator Jacob Javits has, in fact, recently come out in favor of legislation requiring private pension plans to make some provision for cost-of-living increases for retirees. Still another possibility if this is not done within private pension plans is that there will be more and more pressure for expansion of the social security program as to its benefit level, which will then result in the decline of private pension plans and the loss of their unique contribution to the nation's economic development, and even its character.

Index by Persons and Organizations

Index by Subjects

*This book has been set in 11 and 10 point
Times Roman, leaded 2 points. Chapter
numbers are 14 and 30 point Helvetica and
chapter titles are 18 point Helvetica Bold.
The size of the type page is 27 by 45 picas.*